SEEING STARS

McDonald Observatory:
Its Science and Astronomers

BY MARK G. MITCHELL

With Illustrations by the Author

Consulting Editor, Chris Sneden, Ph.D.,
Department of Astronomy, University of Texas at Austin,
McDonald Observatory Staff

EAKIN PRESS ★ Austin, Texas

Dedicated to the memory of my father,
William E. Mitchell,
who first told my brothers and me about stars,
and to the memory of
Dr. Harlan J. Smith,
who gave me my second introduction to astronomy.

FIRST EDITION

Published in the United States of America
By Eakin Press
A Division of Sunbelt Media, Inc.
P.O. Drawer 90159
Austin, TX 78709
email: eakinpub@sig.net

2 3 4 5 6 7 8 9

ISBN 1-57168-117-5

Library of Congress Cataloging-in-Publication Data

Mitchell, Mark.
    Seeing Stars/McDonald Observatory: Its Science and Astronomers / by Mark G. Mitchell.
        p.   cm.
    Includes bibliographical references and index.
    Summary: Relates the history of the McDonald Observatory in West Texas, and discusses astronomical discoveries related to stars.
    ISBN 1-57168-117-5
    1. McDonald Observatory—History—Juvenile literature.
    2. Astronomers—United States—Biography—Juvenile literature.
    [1. McDonald Observatory—History. 2. Stars. 3. Astronomy.]
    I. Title.
QB82.U62F675 1997
522'.19764'934—dc21   96-50011
                                                                              CIP
                                                                               AC

Cover photo courtesy of McDonald Observatory.

The research and writing of this book was made possible in part by funding from the City of Austin Cultural Arts Program and grants from Texas Crushed Stone Corporation and from Wenzel Associates, Inc.

CONTENTS

FOREWORD

You are about to leave on an adventure, a journey through land and sky. Without leaving your chair, through the pages of this marvelous story you will read of how people who loved the stars had a dream. How can we build an observatory, and study the stars, from the darkest sky anywhere in the United States? You will also learn about the nature of their dream; information about the sky and its stars that will last you for years to come.

That dream became a reality more than a half century ago. McDonald Observatory is located near the small town of Fort Davis, Texas. In order to reach it you need to travel along Interstate Highway 10 through some of the most remote parts of Texas, then head south along a narrow, winding road for another hour until, out of nowhere, you see the gleaming domes of the observatory. It is a place where professional astronomers study the sky, make new discoveries, and learn new things about the universe.

McDonald is also a place where amateur astronomers meet professional astronomers. In 1979 Deborah Byrd, then working for the observatory, began a tradition called the Texas Star Party, where amateur atronomers—people like you who observe the night sky just because they enjoy it—could share the sky from this delightful spot. Although the Texas Star Party has changed sites twice since those days, the tradition remains—get the best telescope and the best sky, and see what's up there. It is a dream shared by all who long to study the sky.

I hope that this book will help start you on a journey of exploration and discovery. That is exactly how I started. In 1965 I read how Leslie Peltier, an amateur astronomer who had discovered new comets, had visited the McDonald Observatory site in the mid-1930s. There was no observatory then, just a big concrete pier pointing toward the sky. Leslie saw the dream that night—dark sky, stars

An observer surveys the Davis Mountains from the catwalk of the dome that houses the 82-inch telescope. **McDonald Observatory Photo. Courtesy Tim Jones.**

and galaxies, and a future observatory—and when I read his words I wanted the same thing. I began searching for comets that year. Twenty-one comet discoveries later, I still love the time of day when the sun has set, twilight is fading, and the night sky is preparing for another show. May the hours you spend with Mark Mitchell's book lead you, too, to the stars.

DAVID H. LEVY

World-renowned amateur astronomer; co-discoverer of the Shoemaker-Levy comet, which crashed repeatedly into Jupiter

PREFACE

I am delighted that this wonderful book about McDonald Observatory exists. It tells about what we do here and how we do it. It also talks about the people who work here and what it's like to do astronomy.

In any reasonably clear and dark place it is possible to see the stars and to wonder about the universe without using any equipment other than your eyes and brain. In my experience, many of the people I know who have technical careers began with an interest in astronomy.

Understanding astronomy better makes the universe even more beautiful and more awesome. It is amazing to me that when one sees the fuzzy patch in the constellation Andromeda, which is the center of the giant spiral galaxy M31, one is looking at light that left M31 about 2.2 million years ago, and one is seeing that galaxy not as it looks now, but as it looked then. More distant objects are seen at even earlier stages.

It also amazes me to realize that the universe is believed to have been born in a giant explosion roughly 12 billion years ago and that we think we know the universe's original composition. We have learned that initially there was no carbon in the universe. So the carbon, which makes our life possible and makes all life we know possible, was not always here. It was formed in the cores of stars that have existed since the universe formed, but died before the sun formed.

I hope that you enjoy learning more about McDonald Observatory and about astronomy. If you haven't already done so, I hope that you will visit the observatory. I would like us to share a life-long love of astronomy.

FRANK BASH
Director
McDonald Observatory

JOHN MCDONALD HAD A DREAM

Nobody knew exactly how rich John McDonald of Paris, Texas, was. He wore a slouchy hat. His plain clothes were rumpled and looked slept in. He had never married, so no wife ever told him to change his shirt, get a haircut, or trim his eyebrows.

The only light in his house came from candles and oil lamps. This was the 1920s, so it was possible to hook up to electric lights in Paris then. But Mr. McDonald thought that artificial light was wasteful.

He owned a car, but he kept it in his garage most of the time. It stayed cleaner that way. He preferred his horse and buggy anyway.

He shod his own horse. He mowed his own yard and pruned his own trees. He raised his own goats and bees.

He was what you might call a penny pincher, which was an excellent quality for a man who owned three banks.

After work all day in his office he retreated to his house to read. It was easier for him to be with books than with people. He kept a large library of mostly science books. On some clear nights, neighbors would see him setting up a little telescope in his backyard. He loved to gaze at the stars.

"George," John McDonald told his barber on one of those rare days when he got a haircut. "Someday, they're going to make a telescope so big that we'll be able to see right into the pearly gates of heaven with it."

He invested the banks' growing profits in real estate, cattle, corn, and cotton. But he told people that astronomy was a more interesting subject than business, and much more important than making money.

His listeners thought, "That's easy for him to say. He owns three banks!"

John McDonald died in 1926 at the age of 81. Now for the first time everyone knew how rich he was. He left his fortune—$1.3 million—to The University of Texas in Austin for a single purpose: to build an observatory "for the promotion and advancement of astronomical science."

McDonald's nephews, nieces, and other relatives were stunned. They banded together and went to court to challenge the university's claim to the money. Uncle John was leaving *their inheritance* to The University of Texas to build a . . . *what?*

This was not a reasonable last will and testament, they argued. Uncle John was not of sound mind when he wrote it, they claimed. Well, looking back, you had to admit there had been signs all along: His eccentricity. His aloneness. The uncaring way he dressed. And those strange musings about peering into heaven with a telescope.

University of Texas officials didn't know much about observatories. But they knew to fight for that $1.3 million. A gift like that didn't come along every day. So they found an astronomer from the University of Chicago to testify about how useful an observatory could be for the state of Texas.

Why, you could not find a saner or more practical subject than astronomy, the Chicago astronomer wrote to the court. Without using the stars, you couldn't survey your property, tell the time, or find your way across the sea!

After two trials and four years of legal quarreling, The University of Texas and McDonald's relatives settled on a compromise. The university was left with just enough money ($840,000) to get into the practical business of astronomy.

At least 15 locations from El Paso to Galveston were considered for the new observatory. The site finally selected was a remote mountaintop in southwest Texas, north of Big Bend. Construction finished in the spring of 1939.

Now astronomers from around the country, and about 130,000 visitors per year, drive up to McDonald Observatory to gaze "into the pearly gates of heaven." John McDonald would have liked that.

1 OF MOUNTAINS AND MATTER

THE "HANDS-OFF" SCIENCE

We live in a great city of stars called a **GALAXY**. The word "galaxy" actually comes from an ancient Greek word, *"Galakt,"* which means milk. That's because when Greek shepherds and herdsmen looked up and saw the river of starlight in the night sky, it made them think of milk. The white river was the light of stars in our own galaxy.

There are at least 100 billion of them, although no one has ever counted them all.

Scientists say our galaxy, the **MILKY WAY**, is shaped like a fried egg, and is about 480 quadrillion (480,000,000,000,000,000) miles wide. To give you an of idea of the size, imagine reducing the scale enough to fit our Sun and nine planets—our solar system—inside a teacup. Our Milky Way, or the table on which the teacup sits, would be about the size of North America!

Only 80 years ago, most scientists who studied the stars thought our Milky Way was the only galaxy in the universe. Now we know there are at least 50 *billion* of them. The *nearest* galaxy to our own Milky Way, the Andromeda Galaxy, lies 10 sextillion (10,000,000,000,000,000,000,000) miles away.

Scientists who study these cities of stars are called **ASTRONOMERS**. Their study of the universe is called **ASTRONOMY**.

Chris Sneden, an astronomer on the staff of the McDonald Observatory, said that of all the physical sciences, "Astronomy is the one that never performs an experiment." Why not? Because astronomers can't get their hands on the objects they want to study. The objects are too far away.

The nearest star to our planet (after the Sun) is **PROXIMA**

CENTAURI. It lies 25 trillion (25,000,000,000,000) miles away. It would take the fastest commercial jet from Earth *four million years* to reach it!

Humans won't be traveling to a star any time soon. We don't know how.

"I'd love to go up to a star I'm looking at, take a scoop of its material and bring it home. But I cannot do that. It just isn't possible. We only observe," Sneden explained.

Astronomers can only look. And all they can see is light. Everything they must know is in a pinpoint of light trillions of miles away.

Looking toward the center of our Milky Way, in the constellation Sagitarius. The diagonal line of light is a meteor falling during the camera's time exposure. **Taken from the Hubble Space Telescope. Michael Rich, Kenneth Mighell, James Neill, and Wendy Freedman. NASA.**

High up in the Davis Mountains where the hawks fly, some men camped. They looked different from the ranchers and settlers who lived in the region in that year, 1933. They talked and behaved like city people and had an odd way of camping. They slept through the day and stayed up all night.

There was no road to the top of any of these peaks. The men had to hike. The mountain they were on stood 6,827 feet high—a quarter of the way up in the Earth's atmosphere.

One hundred million years before, these mountains had been volcanoes and gushing lava flows. Now hawks, along with vultures and swallows, made their homes in the red rock and oak, pine, and cottonwood trees that dressed the base of the range. Rattlesnakes hid among the cactus. Squirrels played amid boulders and scrubby

Texas' highest road leads to the top of Mt. Locke, home of the McDonald Observatory in the Davis Mountains.
—McDonald Observatory Photo.

trees. Javelinas, antelopes, and mule deer nibbled the sage and thumped their hooves on the sand.

Below the summits lay the small town of Fort Davis. At an altitude of 5,050 feet it was the highest town in the state of Texas, and maybe the most lonesome.

Fort Davis was so remote from the rest of the state that El Paso, the nearest city, was 175 miles away. Even today, in satellite pictures taken at night, the region appears darker and more empty than about any other area in the United States.

When the strangers camping on the mountain came down into town to buy groceries, residents watched them closely. They weren't hunters. They seemed terribly educated, like college professors. Several spoke with foreign accents.

Finally the campers introduced themselves. They were University of Chicago astronomers. One, a Russian native, was Otto Struve, head of the University of Chicago's Yerkes Observatory. Struve and his colleagues were in the mountains taking readings of the night sky.

The men were dazzled by what they saw up there in the Davis Mountains. So many stars, so many suns filled the night. They shone so fiercely and seemed so close that a visitor might try to throw his hat and hit a few of them.

THE FOREIGNER

You could say that Otto Struve had stars in his blood. His father was an astronomer. His grandfather had been an astronomer. His great-grandfather had been an astronomer. Even his uncles were astronomers! Struve himself was trained to follow in their paths, but he had come of age in what were turbulent, violent times for Russia. He had to put science aside to fight as a soldier in the Russian Civil War in the early 1920s. When his side, the White Army, lost, Struve was in danger of being caught and killed by the revolutionary Red Bolsheviks. So he fled his homeland for a neighboring country, Turkey.

The University of Chicago, a private university funded mainly by the wealthy Rockefeller family, learned of Struve's plight. When officials located Struve, he was still a refugee in Turkey, digging ditches for wages.

Struve was hired to work at the university's Yerkes Observatory. He worked hard, rose in the ranks, and was soon promoted to observatory director.

The Yerkes Observatory owned the largest refractor telescope in the world. Yet Struve and other astronomers who worked there felt frustrated. The observatory was located in Wisconsin, where winters lasted half the year. Fog, clouds, or snowfall often blocked the telescope's view. On nights when the weather was good, the light from so many nearby cities and towns made it impossible for the astronomers to see the night sky well.

Astronomy was difficult at Yerkes Observatory.

Meanwhile Struve and other Chicago astronomers were advising The University of Texas (UT) about the observatory it wanted to build. Struve could not get Texas out of his mind. The University of Texas was not a particularly famous or important school, and Texas was a poor Southern state. But it was rich in clear blue skies.

Struve proposed an idea: Since The University of Texas had no astronomers, why couldn't the two schools team up? UT could build the observatory in Texas. Struve would show them how. The University of Chicago astronomers would operate it for UT.

The agreement was struck.

In no time Struve and other Chicago astronomers were exploring Texas' isolated back roads (and more than a few places without roads). After dark they would pitch camp, pull telescopes out of their packs, and study the night sky. They were looking for the highest and darkest place to see the stars at night.

Of all the vast, wild places in Texas, the Davis Mountains were starting to look the best.

The citizens of Fort Davis grew used to astronomers visiting their town and their mountains. Some residents would even hike up to eat chow with them around an early evening campfire. Some of them once met Mrs. Struve, who joined her husband for a weekend of camping.

Meanwhile Struve was putting pencil to paper. He was roughing out an observatory design and figuring out how, with McDonald's money, the two universities could build the second largest telescope in the world.

5

We think of astronomers being interested in really large objects, like planets or stars. But actually astronomers study the smallest units in nature. They point telescopes at planets and suns. But what they look for are **ATOMS**.

Atoms are the building blocks of nature. They make up suns and planets. They also make up animals, plants, trees . . . clouds in the sky . . . our bones, blood, and muscles . . .

Atoms are so small that a drop of water contains 100 billion *billion* of them. The plastic wrap you sometimes wrap your lunch sandwich in is about 100,000 atoms thick. The simplest and smallest atoms in the universe, hydrogen atoms, are so small that a million of them lined up side by side would not measure as thick as the page you are reading right now.

Scientists have identified more than 100 distinct kinds of atoms. They're called the **ELEMENTS**.

Here's an important element: oxygen. It makes up 21 percent of the mass of the air we breathe. It's nearly 90 percent of the mass of the water (H_2O) in our seas. Oxygen makes up about half of the Earth's crust and 65 percent of our bodies. It is the most common element on Earth.

But not in outer space. In outer space the most abundant element by far is hydrogen. Hydrogen drifts in gigantic clouds throughout the known universe. It provides fuel for the stars.

Some elements are gases, like hydrogen, oxygen, nitrogen (which makes up the rest of the air we breathe), helium and chlorine. Only two elements are liquids—mercury and bromine. All of the other elements are solid. Carbon, silicon, sodium, and sulphur are solid. The metals iron, aluminum, lead, gold, silver and tin are solid elements.

Every atom has a **NUCLEUS** or center that consists of one or more tiny particles called **PROTONS**. Each proton holds a positive electrical charge. An even smaller particle, called an **ELECTRON**, circles the atom's nucleus and carries a negative electrical charge. An electron whirls around the nucleus faster than we can see or even imagine.

For an atom to be comfortable, its positive charges and its negative charges must balance each other. Remove an atom's electrons and you may see sparks.

You've seen this before. The next time you run a comb through your hair, see if you create some static electricity. You'll know when you do, because your hair will stand up and seem to be attracted to the comb. You have raked electrons away from atoms in your hair and your hair is now hungry for the negative electricity in your comb. You have electrically destabilized some of the atoms in your hair!

The nuclei of most atoms contain particles called **NEUTRONS**. A neutron carries no electrical charge at all. Its only job is to act as part of the glue that holds protons together.

Hydrogen, the simplest element and the basic building block of the universe, has only one proton in its nucleus. One lonely electron spins around it.

Pretend you could enlarge a hydrogen atom so that its proton was the size of a grass seed. If the proton was the size of a seed, then the electron's orbit around it would be the size of a football field. The electron itself would be a tiny spark at the edge of the field, too small to see.

If you think this makes the hydrogen atom sound like a lot of nothing, you're right! Atoms are mostly empty space. Still, the electron whirls around the "football field" so fast (billions of times every one millionth of a second, actually) that this energy gives the hydrogen atom a "form."

The kind of element an atom becomes is determined by the number of protons, or positive charges, its nucleus contains. Chemistry is a counting game. In chemistry, numbers don't just describe the atom. Numbers *are* the atom!

For example: A *hydrogen* atom is formed by one proton (a positive electrical charge) and one electron (a negative charge).

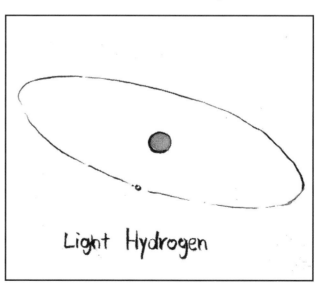

Light Hydrogen

7

✚ Add a proton (and an electron, to make sure the atom stays electrically equalized) and the element changes to **helium**, a very different substance.

✚ Add another proton (and another electron to balance the positive charge) and the helium becomes **lithium**—a new element.

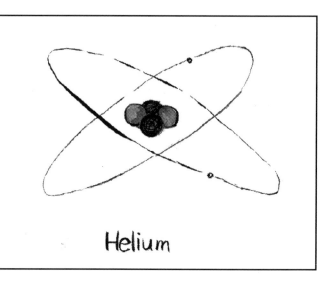

Helium

✚ Add a fourth proton (and an electron for balance) and you create the element **beryllium**. You may never have heard of this one. It is rather rare. It is also nothing like lithium, helium, or hydrogen.

✚ Add another charge to the nucleus and another orbiting electron and you transform the element into **boron**. That makes five protons and five electrons, if you're counting.

✚ Add another proton (for a total of six protons, six electrons) and you get **carbon**.

✚ Add another proton (and another electron) and the result is **nitrogen.**

✚ Add another positive charge to the nitrogen nucleus, and you get **oxygen** (eight protons and eight electrons).

The principle applies all of the way up to the element **uranium**—the heaviest and most complex atom. Uranium juggles **92** protons while **92** electrons whiz around the atom's center!

So, strange as it may seem, the sensory details of our natural world—the features, colors, textures, tastes, and odors—are determined by the number of positive charges bundled in the nuclei of atoms.

Atoms have been around for a long time. Even the atoms that make up your skin existed billions of years before you were born.

The simplest atoms, hydrogen, helium, and a small bit of lithium, were created in the **BIG BANG** explosion that is believed to have started up the universe.

All of the rest of the atoms were made by stars.

ISOTOPES

Neutrons keep company with protons in the nuclei of atoms. A neutron has about the same mass as a proton, but carries no electrical charge at all. Each kind of atom must have its own set number of protons—but the number of neutrons can vary. When atoms with the same number of protons have different numbers of neutrons, the atoms are called *isotopes*.

A carbon atom will always hold six protons. But it can hold six or seven neutrons and still be carbon. (The carbon atom with seven neutrons is just a bit heavier than the one with six neutrons.) The element nitrogen must contain seven protons. But it can have seven or eight neutrons. Uranium never fails to have 92 protons. But one kind of uranium atom carries 146 neutrons, while another kind carries 143 neutrons. These carbon, nitrogen, and uranium atoms are examples of isotopes.

The top of the mountain looked like a gypsy camp. Workers and their wives lived in tents around the construction site, glad to have jobs in the worst days of the Great Depression of the 1930s. In the face of constant wind and intense sun they were building the dome that would house the telescope.

Fort Davis lay nearby, at the base of a cliff wall called Sleeping Lion Mountain. The town had begun as a garrison from where the U.S. Army protected freight supply and wagon trains on the road to El Paso.

African American infantry soldiers whose specialty was Indian fighting had once lived here. The short curly black hair on their heads reminded Comanche and Apache Indians of the hair on a buffalo's back. So the Indians called these troops "buffalo soldiers." But that was two generations before the first astronomer set foot on Mt. Locke. Now the old post lay abandoned and in ruins, and there was not an Apache, Comanche, or, for that matter, an African American to be seen in the town.

Curious visitors from all around West Texas made their way up Mt. Locke to see the dome being built and maybe catch a glimpse of a real astronomer. As a result of so much interest, the astronomers gave weekly public lectures about astronomy. They announced discoveries they were already making with the outdoor telescope they had set up on the mountaintop.

One night an astronomer told the crowd of an astronomical event that had happened in their own backyard. A basin rimmed by mountains called the Sierra Madre, between Fort Stockton and Marathon, was created when an **ASTEROID** smashed into Earth more than 100 million years before! The crater measured nine miles across. Here was a good reason for astronomers to study the sky— to watch out for asteroids like that one!

Lecture nights became so popular they were moved to the high school auditorium in Alpine.

Finally, 1,600 miles away from Mt. Locke, the mirror was ready. For two years workers in a precision machine tool factory in Ohio had polished its glass down to meticulous specifications. Shaped as

The telescope tube being carried by truck up to the top of Mt. Locke.

a disc with a diameter of almost seven feet (82 inches), it weighed nearly two and a half tons.

A train carried the mirror to the Davis Mountains. It was then hauled by truck up to the top of Mt. Locke while the astronomers held their breath. Workers hoisted it into the large dome with pulleys and carefully lowered it into the telescope tube.

The year was 1939. A newspaper headline proclaimed, "LAND OF JACKRABBITS AND SCRUB OAKS BECOMES MECCA OF U.S. SCIENTISTS."

The United States didn't have many astronomers back then. But most of the atronomers in the country traveled to Mt. Locke for the dedication ceremony.

The 82-inch diameter telescope mirror being hauled up into the dome.

CLOUDY SPACE

Clouds go hand in hand with the stars. The clouds in space aren't made of water vapor, as Earth clouds are. Instead they are mostly hydrogen and helium—two gases that have floated around in the universe since the Big Bang. Some clouds also contain microscopic dust—sand, salt, minerals. This dust was blown into space from hot stars that ejected their outer layers, or exploding stars called **SUPERNOVAE**. The dust may contain atoms or chemical **MOLECULES** (more than one atom clumped together). The molecules may contain atoms of silicon or carbon or atoms of metal like iron or gold or uranium. (These last two atoms are made at the instant that a large star blows up. The star that minted these metals is long gone, but the atoms are still drifting in space.)

Clouds of atoms may span trillions of miles. Some of these clouds hum with low frequency radio waves. Others glow with their own light. How? Here's how: Fiery stars inside the clouds heat up electrons in the cloud's gases, causing them to emit colored light.

Some clouds behave like chandeliers in a dining room. They reflect the light of stars inside them.

Some clouds in space block out starlight. Astronomers can't even see the center of our galaxy, where most of the Milky Way's stars are, because so much dust and gas block the view.

Astronomers call all of these clouds in space **NEBULAE**. That's the plural form for an ancient Greek word, "**NEBULA**," which means "cloud."

The Crab Nebula, in the constellation Taurus, marks the spot where a single star blew up more than a thousand years ago. Chinese astronomers wrote that the flash of the explosion stayed in the daytime sky for three weeks. The light, while it lasted, was so bright that it cast shadows, so they said. Arabs, Japanese, and Native Americans saw it too. Today the remnant of the explosion is a beautiful reddish cloud that is still expanding out into space at speeds of nearly *600 miles a second.* (See photo in color photo section.)

The night sky is filled with nebulae. Astronomers are crazy about them, because stars are born inside of them.

Generally, nebulae just hang in space, like smoke after fireworks. But every so often one gets startled, or, as astronomers like to say, "perturbed." Another cloud may bump into it. Or a nearby star may flare up, or blast itself to smithereens. The shock wave from any of these events can push gas and dust together. Pieces of cloud may begin to slowly, lazily rotate.

Over time, an amazing force—**GRAVITY**—compresses these turning fragments.

Gravity is everywhere. Somehow the more mass an object has, the more it wants, and so it bends and shapes the space around it to attract nearby objects to it. Gravity is what holds your feet to the

Earth. The Sun's gravitational pull keeps our solar system from flying apart.

Gravity holds galaxies together. It also pulls the atoms of a nebula into a star.

Over hundreds of thousands of years, it presses the cloud wisp into a knot of hot, spinning gas. This is the beginning of a star. Our Sun formed this way. It has not stopped spinning since then. It has slowed down a bit, so that it rotates only once every 25 days. That's still a fair clip for an object with a diameter of 865,000 miles!

What material in a cloud gets compressed? The basic ingredients you already know: hydrogen and helium, with a sprinkle of other atoms—leftovers—thrown out into space long ago by old or dying stars.

As gravity presses the knot of gas inward, atoms jam into each other at the center. Trapped atoms crowd together. With nowhere to go, they bounce and jump around. Soon they're careening into each other like slam-dancers near the concert stage. Friction from all this crowded moving generates heat. The faster the atoms bounce and jump, the hotter the center becomes.

It's really pretty miserable for the atoms, but gravity doesn't care. It keeps squeezing, producing more friction and heat until eventually the spinning ball of gas glowers like the inside of a furnace. As it twirls, this radiant ball puffs up several sizes. Atoms pulverize each other in the ball's core. Temperatures soar. But gravity, nature's most relentless force, doesn't stop. It keeps shoving, crowding, smashing more atoms into the seething heart of the orb. Something has to give.

And something does. About once every ten days or so in our galaxy, Mother Nature performs one of her most miraculous tricks. A ball of raging hot atoms turns into an engine of creation. And a star is born. (See photo in color photo section.)

Astronomers chow down chuckwagon stew at the observatory dedication cookout.

AJTRONOMERJ IN JTETJONJ

For the first few years, astronomers on Mt. Locke had it almost as rugged as the buffalo soldiers. They endured the isolation and high altitudes. The air was thin enough to make a new visitor to the mountain dizzy. Steady winds combined with a searing sun to chap hands, face, and lips. Nights were cold.

Astronomers lived in the cylinder that supported the telescope dome. It was a bit like living inside a boat, with nautical-looking sleeping quarters, kitchen, a library, and a photographic darkroom. Floors were made of battleship plate steel that clanged with each footstep. Steep stairs led to the telescope on the top floor.

Around the observatory stood a few cabins for workers and engineers. A tiny village existed up on the mountain. Astronomers hauled their water from a well to the dome. A diesel plant generated electrical power. Neighbors included the swallows who built nests in the observatory's crannies and the javelinas who ran across footpaths at night.

For an astronomer or a night assistant, the job at the observatory consisted mainly of staying up all night, taking long-exposure photos of the light of stars, galaxies, nebulae, and other energy sources in space.

Working in the complete dark, he or she checked an eyepiece every few minutes to make sure that the camera or **SPECTRO-GRAPH'S** scopesight was perfectly aimed on the star's light.

When it was time to change observations, an astronomer clambered up to the telescope platform and operated controls to move and re-point the big telescope. Next he'd run to an eyepiece to make sure the telescope and its instruments aimed at the star. Then he ran to change the photographic negative plates in the camera. He negotiated all of this in the dark, sometimes with the aid of a tiny red flashlight. (White light could interfere with the starlight.)

At night in the dead of winter the dome got—and still gets—freezing cold. The interior had to stay the same temperature as outside because heat distorts the telescope image. So on the frostiest nights the astronomer and the night assistant sometimes took turns observing. They staggered shifts—an hour on and an hour off—so each had time to run downstairs to warm hands and feet.

Most nights an astronomer worked alone from sundown to sunup. More than one tired stargazer nearly walked off the telescope platform. Others nearly fell while climbing, in dim red light, to make camera adjustments high above the floor.

It wasn't all hardship. The Chicago astronomers learned to enjoy the silences of the mountain. They took to wearing Stetson hats and the right kind of boots. Some learned to ride horseback.

They taught Fort Davis residents to use the telescope and act as night assistants. In turn, Fort Davis residents invited them into the life of their town. Astronomers became familiar faces at area potluck suppers, outdoor barbecues, and school board meetings.

For the next ten years, McDonald Observatory was one of the busiest observatories in the world. Struve's instincts about where to point the telescope were leading to important discoveries about how stars evolve. Astronomers and engineers came from Mexico, Argentina, Canada, Denmark, Belgium, Holland, Germany, and India.

A STAR IS BORN

Scientists are still learning about how a star forms. But they think they know generally how it works.

Remember the electron of the hydrogen atom? The electron is the negatively charged electrical spark that spins around the atom's nucleus. All atoms have electrons. The simple hydrogen atom has only one. Repeated collisions of a hydrogen atom can knock this spark away, leaving the hydrogen nucleus unprotected, without its electron "shell." Without an electron, an atom is left only with its nucleus and its positive charge.

By the time a star's core reaches a temperature of 10 million degrees Kelvin (the temperature scale astronomers use), nuclei are crashing into each other so often and so violently that a nuclear reaction can begin. It doesn't happen overnight. It took our Sun roughly *30 million years* to reach this stage.

In principle, nuclear **FUSION** sounds simple. Add a proton to the nucleus of an atom and you create a new kind of atom. It's not so simple in practice.

Have you ever tried to push the positive ends of two magnets together? What happens? No matter how hard or how many different ways you try, you can't get them to join up. The ends don't want to meet. They push each other apart. They repel each other.

It's the same with atomic nuclei. Every hydrogen nuclei has a positive charge. When two positively charged particles meet they push each other away, or repel each other.

But at the center of a star, conditions and temperatures have grown so extreme that every once in a while two hydrogen nuclei overcome their electric repulsion. They crash into each other and they stick. They stick so hard that nothing can knock them apart. They **FUSE**.

A glue-like force inside the nucleus of an atom, the Strong Force, has switched on. But it only works at the shortest distances, when nuclei are extremely close to each other.

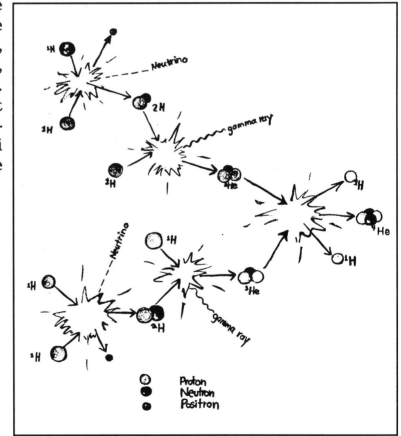

The proton-proton chain reaction.

Ninety percent of the time, most stars and our Sun perform the most common type of nuclear reaction, the **PROTON-PROTON CHAIN**.

When two hydrogen protons fuse, they form a nucleus of **HEAVY HYDROGEN**.

That's Step One.

Step Two is for another proton to slam into this new nucleus and fuse with it. The odds are overwhelming that it won't. But if it does, it changes the heavy hydrogen atom to an atom of **LIGHT HELIUM**.

For Step Three to happen, two light helium nuclei must find each other, beat the odds again, and fuse. (The two nuclei have already made it through Steps One and Two, or they wouldn't be light helium nuclei.) This forms a nucleus of **NORMAL HELIUM**.

A hydrogen atom has changed into a whole new element.

The steps of the proton chain can only happen at the center of a star. Here, conditions are unbelievably dense, temperatures are unimaginably hot, and nuclei bombard each other with a frequency and violence that are truly out of this world.

A dusty nebula in the Pleiades star cluster encloses hundreds of newborn stars like an egg sac. Astronomers even refer to them as star nurseries.

19

Usually when a nebula breaks up or collapses it forms not one but *hundreds* of stars. In time, these stars may pull away from each other and travel in a galaxy alone. But most stay together in pairs (**BINARY STARS**) or in family groups of three or more. Binary stars and **MULTIPLE STAR SYSTEMS** orbit around their combined center of mass like square dancers who hold hands and swing each other around a room. More than half of the stars we see are attached to one or more stars this way.

But not our Sun. It is a partnerless star.

BIRTH OF A PLANET

Remember when the star was just a swirling atom soup? Not all of that gas and dust made it into the final star. A few dust grains and some of the gases were too far out to be pulled into the center. Still attracted to the center, the material kept swirling in a disc around the new star. Eventually gravity compressed it into separate little clumps and knots, forming planets like the one you're on now.

Earth seen from the Moon. Our planet was once just a swirling mixture of dust and gases.

—NASA.

A LIGHT IN THE DARK

The basic nuclear reaction in stars creates helium nuclei. It also sends out the blinding light and scorching heat of our Sun. It lights the Milky Way in our night sky.

This is because when four hydrogen nuclei fuse with each other to become one helium nucleus, a tiny bit of matter escapes as energy.

The helium nuclei is almost one percent (seven-tenths of one percent, to be exact) less massive than the four hydrogen nuclei that crashed to make it.

If you were the kind of scientist who liked to keep track of things, you would want to know, "What happened to that tiny bit of mass that disappeared when the hydrogen atoms formed a helium atom? Where did it go?"

The answer is that each time a nucleus fused with another

nucleus, that tiny bit of mass escaped in a flash. Depending on what step of the chain it happened in, the energy burst out of the nucleus as a **GAMMA RAY** or a **NEUTRINO** or a **PHOTON**.

These are different forms of energy.

It was energy that had helped to hold the original hydrogen atom nucleus together.

MASS is locked-up energy, as the great scientist Albert Einstein showed in his equation $E = MC_2$ (energy equals mass times the speed of light squared). All this means is that the amount of energy a particle contains is proportional to its mass. Mass and energy are the same thing. They're interchangeable. It's that simple. If you know how much mass an object has, you know how much energy it holds. You know how much energy you'll release if you totally destroy that mass.

So as hydrogen nuclei fuse to form a nucleus of helium, a small bit of the energy that was locked up, holding the nuclei together, is set free.

It doesn't amount to much. It was only the energy needed to hold the extra seven-tenths of one percent of mass in the four hydrogen nuclei. It's no longer needed because the helium nucleus is seven-tenths percent less massive. Barely enough energy to raise a housefly off its feet. But it adds up. If you released all of the energy locked in a couple of pounds of hydrogen, the force would be enough to lift a mountain six miles off the ground!

In the core of our Sun, four million tons of hydrogen changes into energy *every second*. No wonder the Sun is so bright! This energy comes roiling and boiling out, spilling, spewing, tumbling, jumping, shooting out of our Sun in particles, waves, beams, and rays. The Sun is 93 million miles away. Even so, its

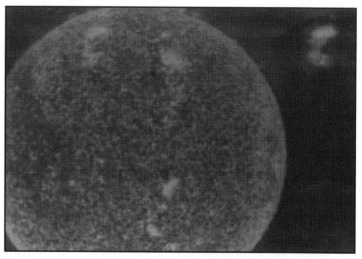

Photo of the Sun.
**—University of Texas
Department of Astronomy.**

radiation can seriously damage your eyes if you look at it for more than a few seconds. Some of this energy we see as visible light. Most of it we cannot see, because our eyes are not built to detect *all* forms of energy.

The proton-proton chain reaction does not start in a star until the star's hottest part—its center—reaches a temperature of 10 million degrees Kelvin (20 million degrees Fahrenheit).

Stars larger than our Sun have hotter centers. In larger stars a second kind of nuclear reaction can occur at the same time as the proton-proton chain. Scientists call this second kind of reaction the **CARBON-NITROGEN-OXYGEN CYCLE**. Like the proton-proton chain, it fuses hydrogen nuclei to create helium nuclei and energy. But it involves more steps and more elements.

As a star nears the end of its life, it runs out of hydrogen to fuse in its center. It has turned it all into helium. When that happens, the star must look for other fuels. When a star's center heats up to 100 million degrees Kelvin, it can start to fuse helium nuclei. This triggers a chain reaction that leads to producing another element, carbon and energy.

If the temperature shoots higher than 600 million degrees Kelvin, which can happen in a really huge star, the star may fuse carbon. A chain reaction from carbon-fusing may result in the elements nitrogen, oxygen, fluorine, neon, sodium, aluminum, magnesium, or silicon, and the release of more energy. Interestingly, none of these elements burn as well as hydrogen, the star's favorite fuel.

At even hotter temperatures, the star may fuse magnesium, silicon, and aluminum for fuel. It will continue to produce new elements and energy. But a star only gets this hot in its final hours. In its dying gasp, a really large star spews all kinds of elements and incredible energy.

When you think of stars twinkling high above in the night sky, you probably don't think of them as big chemical factories in space. But they are. Hydrogen can't build the universe by itself. Stars manufacture the atoms that the physical universe, including our world, is built from.

The by-product of all this atom-making is energy. Or you might say it differently: The by-products of all this energy generation is atoms.

Gravity puts the pressure on the star. It's behind the manufacture of all those atoms and light and energy. It creates the density and heat that lead to fusion.

And once fusion unleashes its awesome explosive power, only gravity's mighty grip keeps the star from blowing to pieces.

So gravity sustains as well as begets the star.

Gravity pushes *in*.
The star pushes *out*.
Gravity pushes *in*.

It's like the overbearing relative who almost hugs you to death. That is just gravity's nature. Only the outward force of a fusing star can stand up to the crush.

The star pushes *out*.

Gravity pushes *in*.

Gravity and the star are locked in a life or death struggle. Like true arch enemies, they need each other. Gravity wouldn't *be* there without the star's enormous mass. And the star requires gravity's compression to fuse hydrogen at its core, to make it a star.

Gravity has held our Sun together for four billion years. But the Sun must keep blasting its mass into energy—or be crunched to a cinder.

PINGING THE MOON

By the 1960s, as America's space program got under way, McDonald's glory days as the world's second largest observatory seemed to be over. Struve was long gone. Larger telescopes were being built. The old McDonald Observatory needed repairs.

University of Texas regents wondered about closing it down. Instead they hired Harlan Smith from Yale Observatory.

Smith was an inspired director. He felt sorry for people who didn't work in astronomy because of all the fun they were missing. Immediately he set about bringing the nearly antique observatory into the space age. He began by establishing an astronomy department at The University of Texas at Austin, so that UT could train its own astronomers.

Next he persuaded the National Space and Aeronautics Administration (NASA), the powerhouse behind the U.S. space program, to help UT build a larger telescope. Smith, like NASA, advocated the human exploration of space. He insisted that if NASA was going to land a man on the Moon and scout the solar system with unmanned spacecraft, it needed the Texas observatory with its **PRISTINE** skies. Besides, it was in the same state as Houston, site of the center which ran the manned space flights.

Smith prevailed. The new telescope, completed in 1969, boasted a main mirror nearly nine feet wide, or 107 inches. Its moving parts alone weighed 160 tons. The new 10-story steel dome that housed it towered over Otto Struve's old dome.

The government put the 107-inch telescope to work gathering information about Mars. Scientists could then figure out how to land the Viking spacecraft there.

NASA used both Struve's and Smith's telescopes to help scientists map the Moon before the Apollo launches.

When astronauts Neil Armstrong and Edwin (Buzz) Aldrin, Jr., walked on the Moon in 1969, they placed on the lunar surface five small reflectors, made of the material you see on highway signs. Astronomers at McDonald Observatory shot giant laser beams through the 107-inch telescope at those markers. The idea was to bounce the laser beams off the tiny reflectors a quarter of a million miles away and try to catch, or detect, them again.

Astronomers "pinged" the Moon with a laser beam in the same way police zap motorists with radar guns to detect speeding cars. They then timed the return of the reflected laser. Since they knew the speed of the laser's travel, they could determine the observatory's distance to the Moon. They saw how, with repeated laser sightings, this distance changed over time. By noting the tiny distance changes, scientists determined the Moon's wobble in space.

—McDonald Observatory Photo—Tim Jones.

Not much light bounced back—about one photon for every ten "pings" of the laser. But it was enough for a sensing device attached to the telescope's eyepiece to register. NASA scientists used these signals to measure a tiny wobble of the Moon's **AXIS**. The wobble told them about the Earth's gravitational pull on the Moon.

2 LIGHT BUCKET

PHOTONS

At the Sun's center two hydrogen nuclei fuse, releasing energy. A radiant particle called a **PHOTON** makes a run for space.

Hydrogen atoms in the way grab and release the photon's energy as it tries to get through. Each time this happens the photon gets whirled around and rerouted in a new direction. The dizzy photon bumps from atom to atom inside the Sun, like a ball in a pinball machine. With so many detours, the journey can take a long time. In fact it can take a photon *a million years* to wriggle from the center of the Sun to its surface. That's a distance of about 430,000 miles.

Once the photon breaks out, it makes up for lost time. It races through space at a speed of 186,000 miles per second—the fastest traveling speed in the universe. If the photon is headed in the direction of Earth (93 million miles from the sun), its light will reach us in eight minutes.

We see some photons from the Sun as visible light. The light is so bright that we must sometimes wear sunglasses. Blue light, which travels in short **WAVELENGTHS**, gets scattered in all directions by our atmosphere. That's why our sky, on a sunny day, looks blue.

Other photons we feel as heat. This is the **INFRARED RADIATION** that warms our planet. The heating creates our wind. It evaporates the water in our seas to make rain.

We may feel the results of other photons a day later—as sunburn! This is from **ULTRAVIOLET RADIATION**, which penetrates our skin.

Extra-high-energy photons from the Sun, like **X-RAYS** and **GAMMA RAYS**, don't make it to the Earth's surface.

The truth is, the photons that shower our planet are only a drop in the vast ocean of the Sun's radiance. The rest of the energy is lost in space. The photons which do make it here are essential to us. Without them, there would be no light on our planet—and no life!

The plants of our world rely on photons to provide nourishment for themselves, animals, and us. Plants use the light to make their food in a process called **PHOTOSYNTHESIS**. As a waste product of photosynthesis, plants release oxygen into the air, which humans and animals require to live.

Photons are behind most of the energy we use on the planet. Photons trapped by plants and trees result in the fuel we burn as coal, oil, gas, and logs in the fireplace!

The ebb and flow of photons to Earth produce our sleep and wake cycles and the seasonal changes.

Finally, for scientists, photons serve one more purpose. They are long distance information carriers. They bring **DATA** from the Sun and other stars. But to receive the news, you need a telescope.

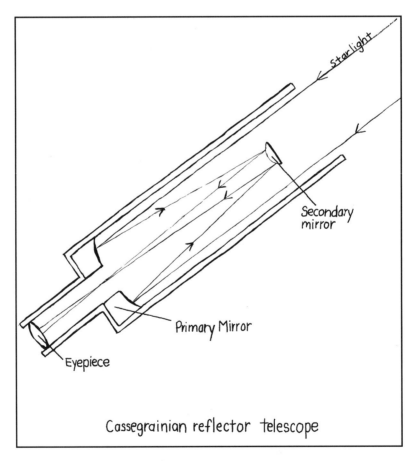

The mirror path of a reflector telescope.

Starlight, which of course includes light from the Sun, contains libraries of information for scientists who know how to read it. A telescope's job is to soak up that light.

Telescopes catch photons like a rain barrel catches rain. The wider the barrel, the more raindrops fall into it. The larger a telescope's mirror, the more photons fall into it.

A big telescope can gather a quarter of a million times more photons from the night sky than our eyes can see.

A **REFLECTOR TELESCOPE'S** large **PRIMARY MIRROR**, which is curved like the inside of a shallow bowl, sees a portion of the night sky. It focuses all the light waves it collects into a big, sharp image and reflects that big, sharp image into a smaller "secondary" mirror set higher in the telescope tube. The secondary mirror returns a condensed picture back down the telescope tube to an electronic camera or another scientific instrument.

A photon travels 186,000 miles in a second. If you multiply all of the seconds in a year, you can find out the number of miles a photon travels in that time, which is 5,870,000,000,000 miles (or about 5.9 trillion miles). For objects very far away in space, such as a star, astronomers sometimes use a **LIGHT YEAR** as a unit for measuring distance. It's much easier to say "one light year" than it is to say "5,870,000,000,000 miles."

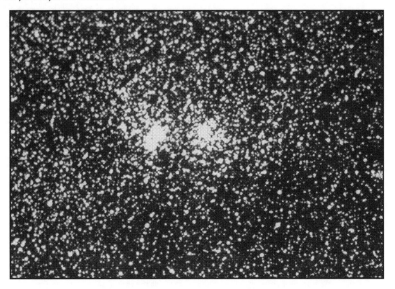

Double star cluster in the constellation Perseus. When we see stars shining at night, it means their photons have made epic journeys of trillions of miles from those stars to our eyes.

—University of Texas Astronomy Department.

If you look at photons one light year away, you see them as they appeared one year ago. When you look at a star *500 light years* away, you're watching that star as it was *500 years* ago. You're looking back 500 years in time. When you look at galaxies *300 million light years away*, you're looking *300 million years* back in time!

So the telescope acts something like a time machine. The telescope mirror is a window that lets us look back into time. The bigger the mirror, the farther back in time you can see. If a telescope was big and powerful enough, it could see back to the day when the universe was born!

IN THE DOME

Even though an observatory telescope is exciting, like a time machine, astronomers don't spend a lot of time peering into one.

Standing in a telescope dome is not like being on the observation deck of the *Starship Enterprise*. There are no dazzling close-ups of planets, no star-spangled panoramas to enjoy (except maybe on posters in the gift shop). Instead you're more likely to see a clutch of cables and wires spilling out of the bottom of the telescope, running along the floor under duct tape, and disappearing into a closed off room in another part of the dome.

Astronomers of today let their gadgets do the looking. That's because human eyes cannot soak up photons like the scientists' cameras do. And human memories can't store information as well as the latest computers.

The popular gadgets of a modern astronomer have included:

• The **CHARGE-COUPLED-DEVICE (CCD)**—This sensitive electronic light detector is no different from the microchip in a home video camcorder. Astronomers attach it to the telescope's eyepiece.

• **CAMERAS**—Once upon a time, before there was television, astronomers relied on ordinary photographic cameras to make long-term film exposures of objects in space. Many hobby astronomers still attach cameras to their telescopes to make beautiful photographs.

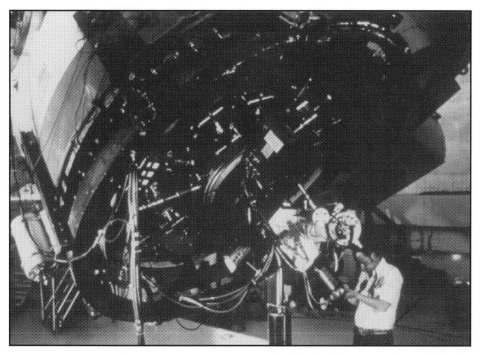

Technician under base of 107-inch telescope.
—McDonald Observatory.

The Harlan J. Smith Telescope.
—McDonald Observatory.

- **PHOTOMETER**—This measures the **LUMINOSITY** of an object in space, or tells astronomers precisely how bright it is. It works just like the light meter in a camera.
- **SPECTROGRAPH**—This instrument separates starlight into all of its separate wavelengths, creating a rainbow or a **SPECTRUM**. Like a tabloid newspaper, a spectrum reveals many of the star's secrets. (For details, see the next chapter.)

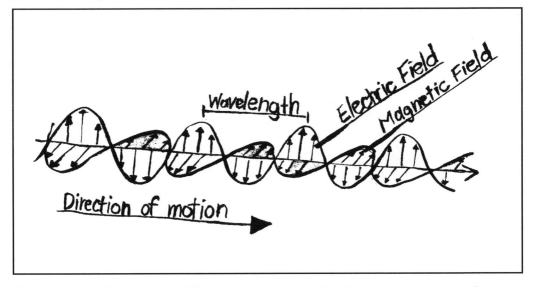

Photons travel in waves. The wavelength is the distance of one cycle, or oscillation, of the vibration. The wave each photon travels stirs up both an electrical field and a magnetic field, which is why a photon's energy is called **ELECTROMAGNETIC RADIATION.**

WAVING AT YA'

All **ELECTROMAGNETIC RADIATION** speeds through space at the same dizzying rate—186,000 miles *per second*. But the waves that move it are all different.

Waves differ by their **WAVELENGTHS**—the distance they take to make one wave motion, or complete one cycle of their vibration. The shorter the wavelength, the more times it vibrates per second and the more energy it carries. The longer the wavelength, the fewer times it vibrates per second and the less energy it carries.

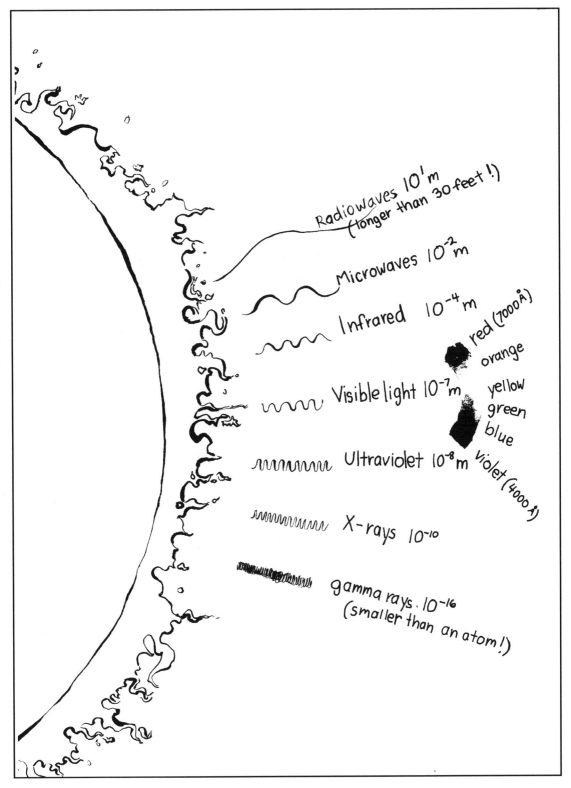

Radiowaves 10^1 m
(longer than 30 feet!)

Microwaves 10^{-2} m

Infrared 10^{-4} m

red (7000Å)
orange

Visible light 10^{-7} m

yellow
green
blue

Ultraviolet 10^{-8} m

violet (4000Å)

X-rays 10^{-10}

gamma rays 10^{-16}
(smaller than an atom!)

The electromagnetic spectrum.

Gamma rays boast the shortest wavelength, with waves much smaller than an atom. These rays **EMIT** dangerously high energy radiation.

Radio waves are among the longest waves and can't hurt you. One single wiggle can span many miles.

Between these two are other kinds of electromagnetic radiation: **X-RAYS**, **ULTRAVIOLET**, **VISIBLE AND INFRARED LIGHT**, and **MICROWAVES**. All of these waves are vibrations from the astounding energy generated by stars.

Our eyes are sensitive to only about three percent of this energy. It's the part of the spectrum known as **VISIBLE LIGHT**.

We see waves of visible light as different colors. Waves that measure less than 4000 **ANGSTROMS** show up as very dark violet. (Angstroms are microscopic units scientists use to measure wavelengths of light. One angstrom is *one ten billionth of a meter!*) Visible light has quite a bit of energy, so its wavelengths are comparatively small. Bluish green light has a wavelength of about 5000 angstroms, for example. Fifty of these wavelengths placed end to end would be about as thick as plastic sandwich wrap.

The longest wavelengths in visible light, approaching 7000 angstroms, show up—to human eyes—as bright red. Between violet and red we find waves of blue, green, yellow, and orange light. All of this light mixed together in equal portions makes pure white light.

THE AMAZING SECRET ATOM DECODER

Chemists know they can learn a lot about a substance by holding it in a flame.

It doesn't matter whether the substance is rock, metal, plant, fabric, chemical solution, or a gas. If scientists examine the light produced by heating or burning a material, they can see what the material is made of. The light will give them the information they need to know.

But to be able to read the messages in the light, they needed a magic light "decoding" device. In the middle 1800s, they came up with one: a **SPECTROSCOPE**.

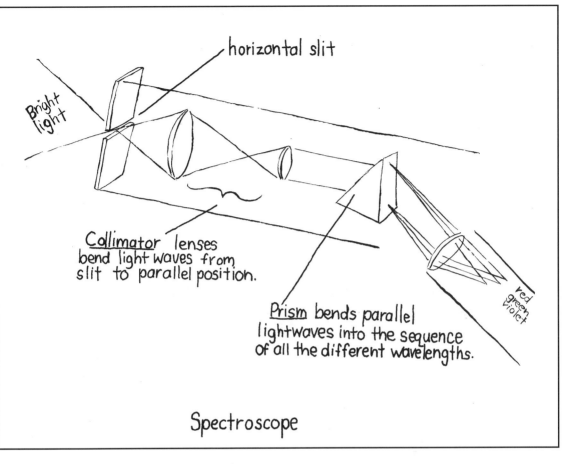

Bright light

horizontal slit

Collimator lenses bend light waves from slit to parallel position.

Prism bends parallel lightwaves into the sequence of all the different wavelengths.

red green violet

Spectroscope

A spectroscope.

A spectroscope spreads out white light into a rainbow pattern of colors called a **SPECTRUM**. You see it when you look into the instrument's eyepiece.

A spectroscope contains a **PRISM**, which is a crystal. A prism unscrambles white light by bending all of the light waves that pass through it. The shortest wavelengths, which make violet-purple light, bend the most. The longest wavelengths, which make red light, bend least. When white light travels through a prism, its wavelengths get sorted out in perfect order from the shortest to the longest.

If you've never seen a crystal or a prism before, you've probably seen a rainbow in the sky after a thundershower. In a rainbow, tiny water droplets act like prisms, spreading out the Sun's bright light into beautiful colors that blend (or perhaps we should say *bend*) into each other. A rainbow is a giant spectrum.

You can also "spread" visible light with a **GRATING**. This is a piece of glass or film celluloid with thousands of lines etched in it. The etched lines bend the lightwaves passing through, just like a prism's angled sides. Some jewelry uses this grated surface to create a shimmery rainbow quality. Mother of pearl (the inside surface of seashells) is a natural grating.

So why do chemists spread light into spectra? Because atoms signal us with light to tell us what kinds of atoms they are. Each element, when it gets hot enough, produces its own special combination of colored light. The colors are amazingly bright and beautiful. They are the purest colors that exist. Chemists can see the element's unique "signature" colors when they heat atoms of the element and view the light with a spectroscope, or a grating.

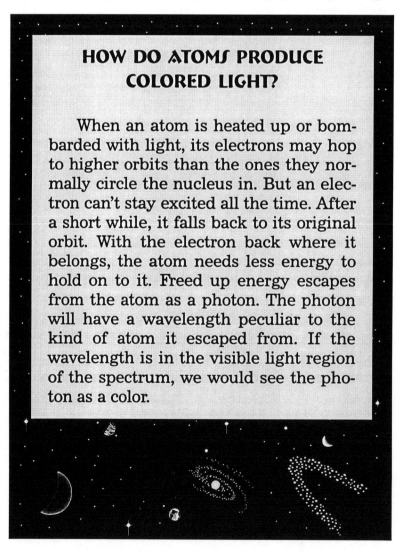

HOW DO ATOMS PRODUCE COLORED LIGHT?

When an atom is heated up or bombarded with light, its electrons may hop to higher orbits than the ones they normally circle the nucleus in. But an electron can't stay excited all the time. After a short while, it falls back to its original orbit. With the electron back where it belongs, the atom needs less energy to hold on to it. Freed up energy escapes from the atom as a photon. The photon will have a wavelength peculiar to the kind of atom it escaped from. If the wavelength is in the visible light region of the spectrum, we would see the photon as a color.

Say you were in a chemist's laboratory and you wanted to look at the colors produced by hydrogen atoms. You would heat hydrogen gas in special vacuum tube until it glowed. Then you would look at it with a spectroscope. Through the eyepiece you would see, against a black background, two stripes of faint, blue-violet light. (Their wavelengths would be 4100 and 4340 angstroms respectively.) You would also see a stripe of pretty blue-green light (a wavelength of 4860 angstroms). And, strongest of all, there would be a thick bright bar of red light (a wavelength 6560 angstroms long.)

These are hydrogen's special wavelengths. These are the colors hydrogen **EMITS** and **ABSORBS**.

Hydrogen emission spectrum.

Helium atoms emit and absorb the following light waves: 7100 angstroms (a red), 6650 angstroms (a bright red-orange), and 5875 angstroms (a yellow-orange).

These are helium's colors.

Helium emission spectrum.

Mercury atoms emit and absorb a strong green light (5460 angstroms), violet light (4360 angstroms), and a weaker yellow stripe. If you've ever flown over a city at night in an airplane, you might have noticed the greenish glow of the city below you. The green is from mercury atoms in the mercury vapor streetlights.

Mercury emission spectrum.

Sodium atoms produce two slightly different yellow-oranges at wavelengths of 5895 angstroms and 5900 angstroms. If you fly over a town at night that uses sodium vapor instead of mercury vapor in its streetlights, you'll see an orange glow.

Sodium emission spectrum.

Calcium sends out two nearly invisible violet lights at 3933 angstroms and 3968 angstroms.

Here's a spectrum pattern for a very heavy element—iron. Look at all the lines! The lines appear throughout the spectrum, in all the colors. Iron sends out and absorbs all of these wavelengths.

Iron emission spectrum.

An element's spectral pattern is like its fingerprint. No two elements have the same pattern. So each atom signals us in a special way. With a spectroscope, you can read an atom's secret code.

Atoms also send and receive wavelengths in the ultraviolet and infrared regions of the spectrum, which the human eye cannot see. Scientists have come up with instruments to detect wavelengths in these regions of the spectrum too.

Even 150 years ago, chemists were experts at matching elements with their spectral fingerprints. They knew most of them by heart. When a substance contained more than one element, chemists could examine its spectrum and pick out the different line patterns for each element in it.

Chemists found something curious when they were playing around with their spectroscopes. When they heated atoms in a gas and put the gas *in front* of a bright flame or light, they saw a different kind of spectrum. Instead of selected bright color stripes against black, they saw a rainbow interrupted by thin black lines in the colors—lines like the bar codes you see on store packages in the supermarket.

The chemists realized that the black lines were actually tiny gaps where wavelengths of light were missing. In fact, they were the same patterns chemists saw in each of the gases' emission spectrum. They were a silhouette, a negative image of the atom's color code.

Atoms absorb as well as emit light. But to be taken into the atom, the light must be of the same wavelength that the atom signals with. A hydrogen atom will only snatch up photons with wavelengths of 4100, 4340, 4860 or 6560 angstroms. These are the same wavelengths that hydrogen sends out when it is excited.

When one of these photons strikes a hydrogen atom, it's like feeding the atom a Wheaties breakfast. The electron in the atom hops to a higher orbit. The atom enjoys a higher energy state for a brief time before the electron drops back to its old orbit. No longer needed, the photon flies out of the atom—but in a path other than the one it originally traveled toward our eyes. From our point of view, the photon's wavelength of light drops out of the spectrum we see. We see a gap where a light wavelength should be.

When chemists saw these gaps in a spectrum, they realized that the atoms in the gas were catching photons coming from the bright light behind it. The atoms momentarily trapped the photons, then spat them out in random directions. The atoms revealed their "true colors," even if it was by showing gaps in their spectra where colors should be.

So chemists can read an atom's color signal two ways. They can heat up a gas and look at it with a spectroscope. In this way they will see a few selected bright individual bars of color. This is what chemists call an **EMISSION SPECTRUM** (because atoms in the gas actually send out light.) Or they can look at the gas in front of a bright light and see the atom's spectrum marked off by black lines, like a bar code, over the colors. Chemists call this an **ABSORPTION SPECTRUM**, because atoms in the gas have absorbed photons with their energies.

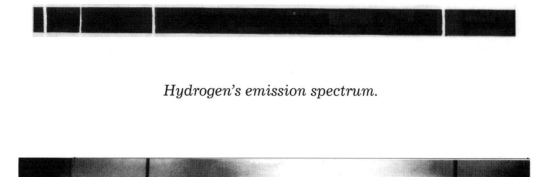

Hydrogen's emission spectrum.

Hydrogen's absorption spectrum.

A spectrum of sodium gas held before a bright light or flame shows absorption lines at 5893 angstroms and 5896 angstroms. Sodium atoms pulled out photons with these wavelengths. They're sodium's yellows—the same yellows sodium produces when it is heated.

Sodium's *emission spectrum* looks like this:

While sodium's *absorption spectrum* looks like this:

Iron's *emission spectrum* looks like:

But its *absorption spectrum* looks like this:

Either spectrum reveals the unique color fingerprints of atoms in the gas. (We didn't print these spectra in color, but their brightness will show the color changes.)

These two different methods of reading an atom's color led to a wild discovery. Read on . . .

KINFOLK

One day in the middle 1800s, two physicists in Germany, Gustave Kirchoff and Robert Wilhelm Bunsen (inventor of the Bunsen burner, the gas burner still used by chemists in their laboratories) turned their spectroscope on the biggest, brightest light they could find—the Sun.

Were they ever surprised! They saw an absorption spectrum. The gaps appeared because atoms on the Sun's surface absorbed photons of certain wavelengths streaming out of the Sun's interior.

The blinding light in the Sun's center, where fusion created energy, was the background light. The Sun's atmosphere, where the gas is thinner and cooler than inside the Sun, acted like the gas cloud in the chemists' lab.

Bunsen and Kirchoff magnified the spectrum so they could see it better. They counted 600 absorption lines. Both physicists recognized line patterns they knew well. They saw common, everyday elements known to chemists everywhere—hydrogen, carbon, oxygen, nitrogen, silicon, and more. It meant these atoms were on the Sun's surface.

With growing excitement, the two Germans tried to identify every pattern they saw in the Sun's spectrum. They could hardly believe their results. Nearly every pattern they found was familiar to them.

This was a breakthrough for astronomy. Scientists had always imagined that matter in space would be unlike Earth's. Unknowable. Alien. The Sun, stars and planets were, after all, out of this world. But here was proof that the Sun was as ordinary and easy to know as a rock in the backyard.

Today scientists believe that if you counted all of the atoms in the sun, you would find that about 92 percent of the number are hydrogen. About 7.8 percent of the total are helium. The remaining .2 percent of the number are atoms of carbon, oxygen, and (in trace amounts) nitrogen, neon, magnesium, silicon, sulfur, iron, and the rest of the elements.

In other words, *the Sun is made of the same chemical stuff that we are.* It's more than a neighbor. It's a relative.

After Bunsen and Kirchoff's discovery, astronomers attached spectroscopes to their telescopes and pointed them at not just the Sun but other stars. Over and over they found the same thing. The stars in the night sky might be larger or smaller, hotter or cooler, or younger or older than our Sun. They might be blue or red or white or yellow or orange or even green. But they are made of the same old atoms.

Astronomers now believe that this is true of all stars—in the *50 billion* or more galaxies that are thought to exist!

ſPECTRAL DE-PUZZLING

Just as chemists train their spectroscopes on all kinds of materials on Earth—from minerals to ashes to fabrics to plants—astronomers aim their spectroscopes at star surfaces, atmospheres of planets, and nebulae in space.

Spectroscopy is central to modern astronomy. With it, we can see the "chemical signatures" of atoms thousands of trillions of miles away.

By analyzing a star's spectrum, astronomers can learn what the star's surface is made of and how much of each element is there.

With these two bits of insight, astronomers can go on sleuthing

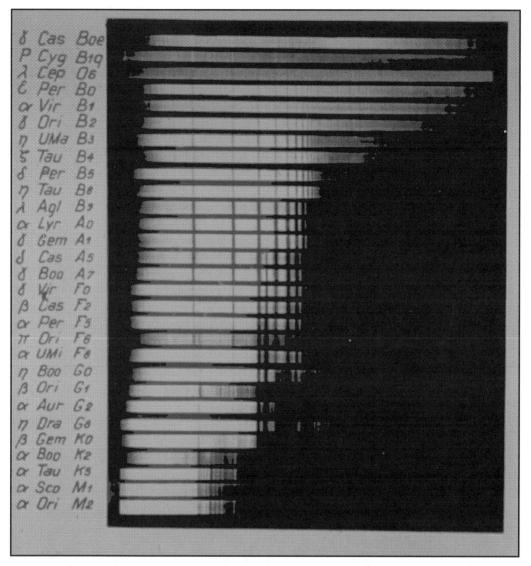

Different stars' spectra. To see spectral lines in better detail, scientists will magnify a spectrum they obtain with lenses. And they may use additional prisms to spread the light's rainbow.

—University of Texas Astronomy Department.

like good detectives to solve one mystery after another about a star. They can make good guesses about what is happening deep inside the star. They can calculate how much gravity a star contains and how hot it is. They can tell if the star is actually one star or two stars circling each other. They can determine how fast the star is rotating and how fast it is traveling through space. A star's spectrum can even tell us if the star is coming toward us or moving away from us.

For example, say you've taken the spectrum of a star. In it you recognize typical element patterns. But there's one big difference. All the "bar codes" appear to have shifted toward the red wavelengths at the far right of the spectrum. It means that the star is moving in a direction away from the astronomer. Astronomers say the light has "**RED-SHIFTED**." That's because when light moves away, its wavelengths *stretchhhh* behind it in a phenomonom called the **DOPPLER EFFECT**. The waves of the receding light actually lengthen between you and the light. The longer the wavelength, the redder the light.

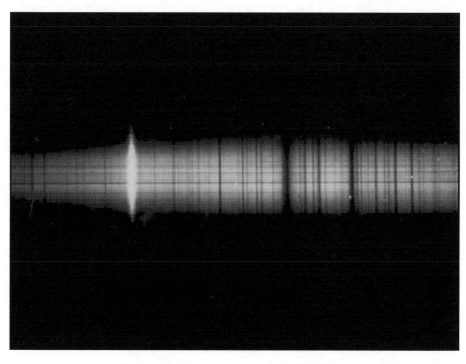

Emission spectrogram of the Sun.
—University of Texas Astronomy Department.

When light moves toward us, its wavelengths bunch up and shorten between the light and us. This actually makes the light bluer. Spectral patterns move to the far left of its spectrum, among the wavelengths of blue-violet light. The light "**BLUE-SHIFTS**."

(It works for sound waves as well as light waves. You may have heard for yourself the high pitch of a train whistle as the train approaches you. Did you notice how the sound drops to a much lower pitch as the train passes you and speeds away from you?)

Most stars and galaxies show "red-shifted" spectrums, which means that they are racing away from us. The wave cycles of their light stretch longer and longer. This led an American astronomer named Edward Hubble to one of astronomy's great discoveries: the universe is expanding.

A LABOR OF LINES

Chris Sneden of Austin knew he would be an atronomer from the day his mother took him to his first planetarium when he was 10. Now he is a spectroscopist for The University of Texas. Ten percent of Sneden's work is gathering light for the spectra of the stars. The other 90 percent is working to disentangle the patterns in their spectra. That's how he determines what the stars are made of.

Dr. Chris Sneden.
—Mark G. Mitchell.

"Give me a Moon rock and I'll wonder whose backyard that came from. You don't give that to an astronomer, you give it to a geologist," Sneden said. "An astronomer knows light. That's the only thing we have to work with.

"But isn't it extraordinary that without being able to handle the objects we look at, we can take the light they choose to send us and figure out the secrets of how they were born, how they live, how they will die, and how they give us the life-giving elements we find on Earth?

"That's the excitement of spectroscopy. We're taking advantage of the fact that atoms and molecules emit and absorb light. They emit and absorb light which is characteristic of their inner structures—for atoms, how they hold their electrons. We can use that—that they emit and absorb light only at certain energies, different wavelengths—to figure out which elements exist out there and how much of each one."

"We look for the patterns that we've memorized of the different wavelengths that the elements emit or absorb. Suppose I'm trying to find out how much sodium exists in the surface of a star. I know that sodium atoms will absorb light at only certain wavelengths or colors over the spectrum. I find those places in the star's spectrum and I look to see how much light is being taken away at those wavelengths. That tells me how many sodium atoms there are in the star," he explained.

"Unfortunately, the pattern of some atoms is very complex. For instance, an atom of iron emits colors and frequencies all through the spectrum. Some elements have emissions or absorptions which fall on top of each other, so it makes a messy pattern.

But you can still do it. It doesn't mean the patterns don't exist. You can still look for the major emissions and absorptions and still identify which elements are there. It just means that we have to do a little work to disentangle all the different elements."

By deciphering the chemical compositions of various stars, astronomers can test their models and theories about how nuclear fusion works to build the elements.

"Fusions of the simpler atoms occur because the masses of the stars crunch them down," Sneden said. "The Sun could not care less that it's doing **ALCHEMY**. All it wants to do is release energy and shine. But the by-product of fusion is the nuclear ashes, and those ashes are all the life-giving elements that we know.

"Stars that were born at the beginning of our galaxy did not have a lot of these ashes. They were composed almost entirely of hydrogen and helium. So when I find a star that has only one thousandth of the fraction of heavier atoms like iron, thorium, sodium, calcium chromium, nickel . . . or any heavy element that other stars have, it signals to me that it was born from a gas that was pretty unprocessed, pretty **PRISTINE**. It often means that I've found a star that was born near the birth of the galaxy."

Sneden's particular interest is a class of stars smaller than our Sun called "Halo Stars," which float just above our galaxy. Because they are so small, they have lived for a very long time. In fact, they are among the earliest stars to have formed in the Milky Way.

"I'd like to know how we got the amount of uranium on the Earth that we got," Sneden said. "How did gold get in the Earth? Is there a logical way that we can show how the elements we use for life were actually created? Can we show how this was done? Mostly, sort of, we've got it figured out. You can trace the sequence of element manufacture by their atomic weights . . .

"But there's much to learn. If I can get reliable chemical compositions of stars at the start of the galaxy, then we can try to trace the sequence up to the formation of the Sun."

THE JUN'J JPECTRUM

Sneden has pinned a spectrum of the Sun to a wall in his office. The spectrum is actually several feet long, but it has been cut up and placed strip above strip, so that it can fit on the wall.

Spectrum patterns made by most elements become second nature to astronomers over time, explained Sneden. He points to an absorption line on the poster. "I know that this is an absorption by hydrogen." He indicates another region. "This whole band of absorption of light is caused by a simple molecule, the CH molecule, consisting of one carbon and one hydrogen atom.

"These broad absences of light here are absorptions of calcium. Here are absorptions of sodium. The more minor absorptions belong to other atoms and molecules." He gestures with one hand. "Iron is literally throughout the spectrum.

"See these absorption bands? These are caused by the Earth's atmosphere. The Earth's atmosphere doesn't let the light of those wavelengths from the Sun reach the ground."

Sneden explains more about the effect of absorption.

"One reason the Earth is warm is that water absorbs infrared light. The visible light from the Sun comes in easily to the ground and heats up the rocks. The rocks emit heat which is infrared light. That heat tries to go back out through the atmosphere. But it is blocked by carbon dioxide and water vapor in the atmosphere. It's called the **GREENHOUJE EFFECT**."

Colors are a fascinating part of astronomy. Sneden continues:

"The blue light of the sky is the scattering of direct sunlight by atoms and molecules in the Earth's atmosphere. If we had no atmosphere, the Sun would look bluer than it does.

47

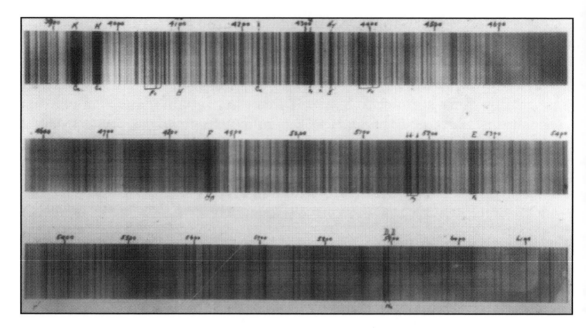

Sun's absorption spectrum. Computers translate spectra into line graphs or bar graphs for scientists to examine. The typical graph shows wavelengths on the bottom and luminosity on the left side. Wavelength emissions or absorptions spike the graph line as it runs across the spectrum.

—University of Texas Astronomy Department.

"As the sun sets, it looks redder as we see it through more of the Earth's atmosphere. The long wavelengths of red have the easiest time getting through, while the blue gets scattered across the sky."

3 FLASHES IN THE NIGHT

THE MOUNTAIN WITH EGGS

Today the top of Mt. Locke looks like a space colony. It is an other-worldly compound at the end of the highest public road in Texas.

McDonald Observatory's two white domes are landmarks in the Davis Mountain range. A Mexican name for Mt. Locke is *"La Montaña con Dos Huevos"* (The Mountain with Two Eggs).

Actually, there are four "eggs" on Mt. Locke. Two small white domes keep company with the two large ones. They enclose telescopes

The white domes of McDonald Observatory at the top of Mt. Locke.

too. Primary mirrors in these smaller telescopes were cut from the doughnut hole of the 107-inch mirror.

In the daytime, the large domes are human beehives. Nearly 50 people work in the offices and workshops that honeycomb them. Workers include engineers, electricians, optics technicians, computer programmers, machinists and mechanics, carpenters, maintenance workers, cooks, cleaning staff, and astronomers' night assistants. Many of them live on or around the mountain.

Self-sufficiency remains a way of life on the mountain. If a truck breaks down, mechanical crews fix it. A machinist on the mountain might even make the part needed. It's a long way to the nearest repair shop.

The astronomers come and go. They are the central purpose of the hive. Everyone labors to support them. Typically, four to seven dwell on the mountaintop at any one time. They might be from Austin, an eight-hour drive away, or from anywhere in the United States. In the daytime they sleep in the "TQ" (**TRANJIENT QUARTERJ**), a dormitory built for them on a cliff under the 107-inch dome.

At night astronomers work in windowless cubbyholes high up in the domes, like astronauts atop a giant rocket. On a clear night they use every telescope on the mountaintop.

After sunset, the mountain is kept dark. Windows in the "TQ" stay shuttered, to keep room lights from interfering with the night sky observations. Even a flashlight can interfere with observing.

Residents of Jeff Davis County and the town of Fort Davis help by keeping their lights low. The instant a high school football game ends, the stadium lights switch off. Streetlights and even private security lights on ranches are fixed with hood covers to shield light from the sky.

The oldest dome on the mountain still has the feel of an old submarine. Rooms where astronomers once slept now house workers, workbenches, desks, and computers. (Some monitors feature "Star Trek" screensavers.) The ground floor has a telephone switchboard, a post office, and a library with a ticking ship's clock and bookshelves encased by steel and glass.

A circular hall on the second floor has more cubbyholes, work stations, and a second library with racks of magazines and paperback books.

Librarian Jane Wiant keeps astronomers supplied with leisure and technical reading materials. "When the astronomers are not working, they *love* to read science fiction," Wiant said. "There's a definite interest in **EXTRATERRESTRIAL** life.

"I always think of scientists as being very factual and not getting particularly excited about the realms of 'what if.' But a lot of them definitely believe that there are beings out there, and they spend their free time studying that."

The fourth floor evokes scenes from a Jules Verne novel. There is the great old Struve telescope, with its notched gear wheel sur-

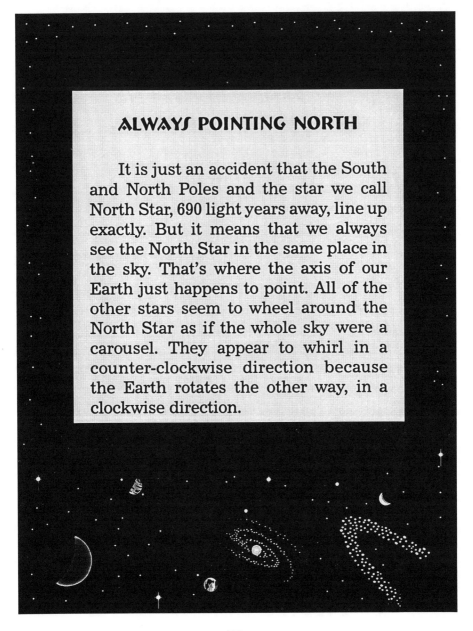

ALWAYS POINTING NORTH

It is just an accident that the South and North Poles and the star we call North Star, 690 light years away, line up exactly. But it means that we always see the North Star in the same place in the sky. That's where the axis of our Earth just happens to point. All of the other stars seem to wheel around the North Star as if the whole sky were a carousel. They appear to whirl in a counter-clockwise direction because the Earth rotates the other way, in a clockwise direction.

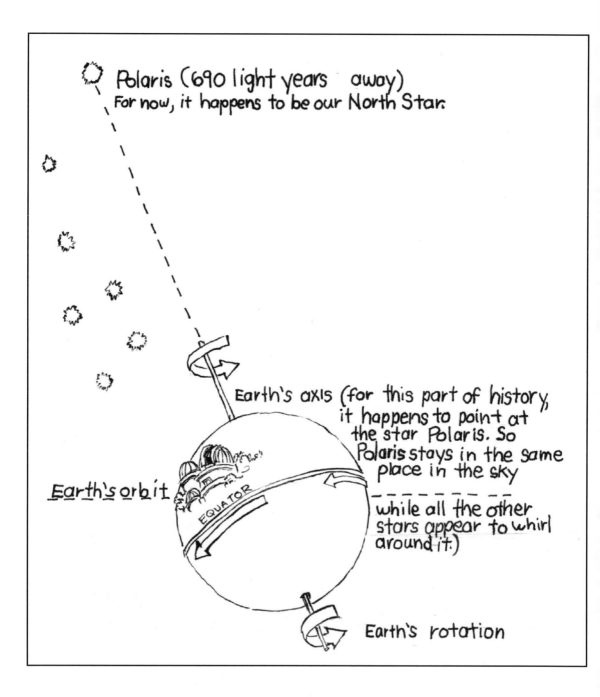

Polaris (690 light years away)
For now, it happens to be our North Star.

Earth's axis (for this part of history, it happens to point at the star Polaris. So Polaris stays in the same place in the sky

while all the other stars appear to whirl around it.)

Earth's orbit

EQUATOR

Earth's rotation

rounded by platforms, stairs, balustrades, and the scuffed steel battleship flooring of 60 years ago. Twenty-six feet long, the telescope pivots on an axle. The axle is mounted on an axis aimed at the North Star. This is how the telescope smoothly tracks stars as they move across the night sky.

The eyepiece of the 1939 telescope is now wired to a silicon chip about the size of large postage stamp called a CCD (**CHARGE-COUPLED DEVICE**). Half a million **PIXELS**, or picture elements, cover the CCD's shiny surface. (CCDs in the larger and newer Harlan J. Smith telescope have four million pixels!)

The pixels in a CCD detect the distant light of stars and galaxies. (Some of this light is tens of millions of times fainter than we can see with just our eyes.) Each pixel converts the light it "sees" into an electrical signal. All of the pixels working together produce an electronic image, just like the pixels on a computer screen. Or like dots of ink make up a photo or a comic in the newspaper. (These are called pixels too.)

The electronic image is beamed into a computer, which automatically translates the image into numbers. Astronomers use these numbers to analyze the image.

Otto Struve and his astronomers would have loved a few CCDs!

MOTION EMOTION

Dr. Art Whipple wears eyeglasses, a short-sleeve shirt, khakis, and loafers. He looks youthful and relaxed behind a computer.

He is an astronomer. But he doesn't point his telescope at a star. "I observe . . . planets, asteroids, comets and satellites [moons], and they *move*," he said.

ASTEROIDS are big chunks of metal or rock. They fly around the Sun in orbits that are often extremely precise. Between Mars and Jupiter, a big "belt" of asteroids circles the Sun.

"The 'asteroid belt' is basically pieces of a planet that didn't form," Whipple related. "I look at asteroids and comets, too, as fossil remnants of our solar system. They're just like dinosaur bones or something.

"The asteroid belt grinds against itself. The pieces have gotten all scattered and broken up and stomped on. What we're trying to do is put them back together, just like a paleontologist would put together dinosaur bones. If you take the orbits and piece them together going backward in time, you can slowly build up a picture of what the early solar system looked like."

When Dr. Whipple travels to the McDonald Observatory, it's usually to track the motion of an asteroid or a comet through space, against the background stars.

Like every other astronomer, Whipple must apply for funds to work at the observatory and to spend time to complete his research project. Then he must apply to the telescope allocation committee.

"You may get the money and not be able to get a date on the calendar to use the telescope. Or you may get the telescope time, but you can't get the funding," Whipple said.

If he is awarded both funding and the use of a telescope, he goes to work to figure out his observing plan. That means, for him, determining first where to point the telescope. "When you're looking at stars, that's not too hard. Stars already have map grid coordinates that telescopes are used to pointing to.

"But when you're looking at asteroids, moons, and comets, and all of the things in the solar system that *move*, you can't always be sure where they will be. It takes some figuring out.

"With planets you can pretty much pretend that they're on a fixed ellipsis, and that will give you a position certainly well enough to plant them in the sky. With asteroids, that's not true. So the biggest job I have is to calculate the position of everything I want to look at for the whole time, for every minute that I want to look at it."

He calculates a position in space where he believes the asteroid should be for each day that he'll observe.

"You type into the computer, 'Where is this object right this minute?' and the computer looks at where it was yesterday and where it is today and where it's going tomorrow. And it figures out where it is *right now* very accurately."

The computer takes into account that asteroids and comets are constantly being tugged by the gravitational pull of all of the planets in the solar system, and in a pretty significant way. Gravitational pull on the asteroid by the large planets, the asteroid's **TRAJECTORY** and rate of speed through space are all keyed into the computer program.

"We numerically integrate the orbits and make a big dynamical model that lives in the computer that actually predicts where the asteroid will be," Whipple said. "That's the main thing I need to do to get ready."

Whipple's specialty—understanding the motions of objects through space—is called **CELESTIAL MECHANICS**.

Like most of the astronomers, Dr. Whipple tries to arrive at the observatory the night before his observing run starts. He rides a commercial airliner from Austin to the Midland/Odessa airport. In Midland he rents a car. He drives southwest into the Davis Mountains, which takes about three hours.

That first night in the TQ, Whipple tries to stay up all night. At sunrise, he goes to bed. He tries to sleep through most of the next day. In the late afternoon, he gets up and walks to one of the small domes with the 30-inch telescope and checks his instruments to make sure they are working and measuring properly. Whipple spends the night observing in a hut filled with computers and instruments off to the side of the dome.

"My last project was observing with the 30-inch and the prime focus camera," he said. "I use a wide field CCD with an electronic camera. It allows me to take a picture of an asteroid or a **SATELLITE** [a planet's moon] against a background of stars. We use that image to measure the positions of objects we're interested in, relative to the stars.

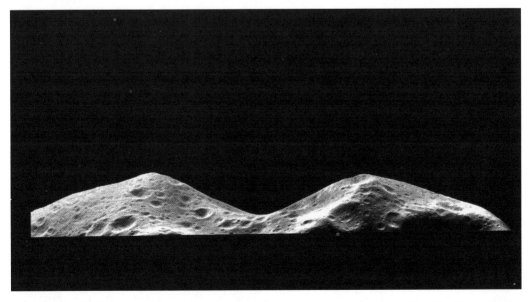

Asteroid 243 Ida, snapped in close-up by a camera aboard the Galileo Probe.
—NASA.

"Whenever an asteroid comes very close to the Earth, it's a wonderful opportunity to observe it."

In February 1996, scientists sent up an unmanned spacecraft to look at Eros 433, an asteroid about twice the size of New York City's Manhattan Island. The space probe was expected to reach Eros in 1999 and orbit it for a year.

NIGHTWATCH

Dr. Guillermo Gonzales, a young astronomer from The University of Texas, sits in a control room that has the feel of a long attic. He watches the numbers flow across computer screens. Occasionally he glances down into a physics textbook propped open on the counter.

When it is time to move the telescope, Dr. Gonzales walks across the room, opens a heavy door, and descends metal stairs into a kind of large cave. The pit is dark but for the red glow of his flashlight and, high above his head, a great window of night sky.

Dr. Gonzales climbs up on to the platform of the old 1939 telescope. He moves a lever and hits some computer keys. The dome ceiling pivots for a new outdoor view. Metal rubs metal with a hair-raising shriek. The dome quakes and rattles in the night wind. To follow the window, the telescope changes angles. The motor that moves it growls hoarsely.

Confident—even regal—as he stands behind the controls on the platform, Dr. Gonzales could be the pilot of a UFO.

Dr. Gonzales sips orange drink in the TQ dining room as he listens for conditions outside to improve. It is midnight, and 40-mile-per-hour winds have interrupted the work of all the astronomers on the mountain.

The dining room is where observatory folk go at night to wait out storms or cloudy conditions. Here they visit and poke around in the astronomers' refrigerator for snacks.

In the daytime, a picture window looks out on the Hobby Eberly Telescope under construction on neighboring Mt. Fowlkes. But tonight, as usual, blinds are drawn. The kitchen is closed. The dining room looks plain with fake-wood paneling and metal folding chairs

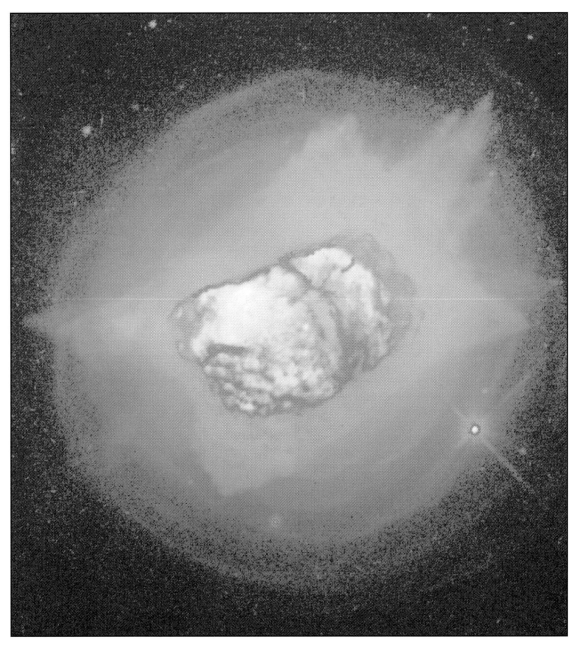

Planetary Nebula NGC 7027. The tiny white dot in the nebula's center is a white dwarf—all that remains of the original star. Its Red Giant phase is long over. Our Sun will be like this white dwarf at the end of its life.

—Hubble Space Telescope, Howard Bond,WFPC2, NASA.

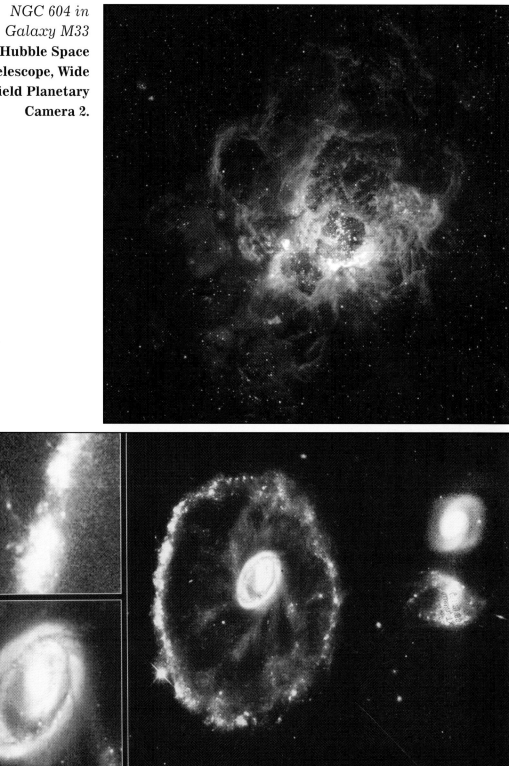

NGC 604 in Galaxy M33 —**Hubble Space Telescope, Wide Field Planetary Camera 2.**

Cartwheel Galaxy —**Hubble Space Telescope, WFPC 2, NASA.**

Below: Dense clouds of molecular hydrogen gas and dust make up the Eagle Nebula. Hidden in the small fingers of these ghostly pillars (as on top of the left pillar) are stars being born.
    —Hubble Space Telescope, Jeff Hester and Paul Scowen (Arizona State University), WFPC2, NASA.

Above: Death of an Ordinary Star— Egg Nebula
—Hubble Space Telescope, WFPC2, NASA.

The Orion Nebula and its Trapezium Stars. Stars condense from the scattered atoms in a nebula, just like raindrops condense from the water vapor in a thundercloud. The process is as natural as rain.

—Hubble Space Telescope, C. R. O'Dell (Rice University), WFPC2, NASA.

and tables. Orange clay pots hold miniature cacti grown by a gardener on the mountain. On the wall is a telephone and one picture—an artist's conception of what the Hobby-Eberly telescope dome will look like.

Dr. Guillermo Gonzales studies R.V. Tauri Variable stars with the 82-inch "Struve" telescope.

—Mark G. Mitchell.

Dr. Gonzales has traveled here from Austin to take the spectra of a special class of older Red Giant stars called RV Tauri Variables. These stars are named after the constellation Taurus, the bull, where the first one was found.

VARIABLE STARS are called variable because their light isn't steady. It varies from light to dim. An R.V. Tauri Variable changes brightness because it **PULSATES**. The star flares up, then shrinks every couple of months in a repeating cycle.

"Basically I observe these stars every month, since their appearance will be a little different from one month to the next," Dr. Gonzales says. "When they swell up, they send shock waves into space.

"My stars are mostly 14 to 15 billion years old. Some of them are found in globular star clusters, which contain the oldest measured stars in the galaxy.

"These stars are special. They are near the end of their life. And they pollute their atmospheres with elements they have recently produced. I'm looking for signs of freshly minted elements on their surface."

Younger stars, or even middle-aged stars like our Sun, hide the elements they manufacture. They hold on to the atoms tightly in their centers as if they were valuable treasures.

A star is opaque, not clear. It is somewhat like a soft white glowing light bulb. It is impossible for scientists to see what is happening inside. So astronomers can't really see the chemical composition changes that happen in fusion. If astronomers could, they would look to see if the star's center was increasing in helium. They would check to see if carbon was giving way to nitrogen. Helium and nitrogen are by-products of nuclear reactions.

"With *young* stars we can't see these changes because the stuff stays down in the interior," Gonzales explains.

Old **RED GIANT STARS** behave differently.

Red Giants throw their elements up to the surface as soon as they make them in a heat transfer process chemists call **CONVECTION**. Think of tomato soup at a "rolling boil" on the stove. Soup from the bottom of the pot rolls to the top then circles back down. Then in the next moment, it comes up again.

In a Red Giant star, the hot gases act like the tomato soup. When the gases roll up from the bottom, they sometimes bring up elements that were just made in the core of the star and dump them on the surface.

By studying the surface, astronomers can find hints of the processes happening in the star's center. For example, if they see a drop in carbon and an increase in nitrogen, it confirms their ideas about how one fusion sequence, the carbon-oxygen-nitrogen cycle, works.

How does an astronomer know when a star is dredging up fresh elements to the surface?

Elements Dr. Gonzales usually finds in his R.V. Tauri Variables are common ones: carbon, nitrogen, and oxygen. But once in a while he detects rare, radioactive metals like technetium.

Technetium atoms are unstable and decay after only a couple of hundred thousand years. Two hundred thousand years ago is *recent* to an astronomer. So when technetium shows up on the star's surface, there is no question that it was made "recently." If Dr.

Gonzales finds technetium in the atmosphere of an R.V. Tauri Variable, he knows that the star is bubbling up fresh elements from its center.

Tipping back the last of his orange drink, Dr. Gonzales says he enjoys driving out to the observatory. "It gets pretty monotonous back in Austin working on the computer every day," he adds.

But tonight he hopes the weather will clear up, so he can go back to the telescope. Earlier, dust threatened to sandblast the telescope's lenses and the 82-inch mirror. The dome's shutters were ordered shut.

"The wind was really rattling the dome. I tried to climb out on the catwalk for a minute and I was nearly blown off," he says.

An astronomer's job may not be as safe as it seems . . .

RED GIANTS

Ordinary stars fuse hydrogen—their favorite fuel, the most common element in space—and convert it to helium. Helium is the next lightest element.

As helium gets made, it accumulates in the center of the star, astronomers say, like ashes in a fireplace. Helium needs much hotter temperatures to begin to "burn." The star is not that hot yet. (Our Sun is at this stage now: fusing hydrogen into helium in its fireplace.)

But as a star nears the end of its life, it runs out of hydrogen fuel. Energy production slows down. So gravity squeezes harder on the star. Friction heats the interior again—enough to fuse a few more hydrogen atoms. But not in the core, where no more hydrogen is left to fuse. Instead, fusion happens in a region surrounding the core called the "shell."

Hydrogen fuses to helium in the shell, generating more "ashes for the fireplace." Energy is released, pushing out the star's outer layers. The star swells. Its core shrinks and the outer envelope expands. Now the star is called an Orange or Red Giant. Many of the really bright stars we see in the sky are **RED GIANTS** or **ORANGE GIANTS**.

Astronomers study Red Giants to test their theories about how nuclear fusion works and how elements are manufactured inside stars.

After spending 90 percent of its life as a medium-large stable star like our Sun, a star changes size. A few billion years from now, when our Sun balloons into its Red Giant phase, it will consume Mercury, Venus, and maybe even the Earth.

A Giant looks beautiful in the night sky, but it's a desperate stage for a star. It means time is running out.

Up to this point, the star has not been hot enough for the helium "ashes in the fireplace" to burn. But now, with gravity pressing harder on the star and hydrogen fusion raging in the star's shell, temperatures in the core shoot past 100 million degrees Kelvin. The "ashes" ignite. Fusion begins. And helium cooks into carbon, the next element in the fusion sequence.

Death of a Star.
—Taken from Hubble Space Telescope.
Raghvendra Sahai and John Trauger. NASA.

Carbon is an even tougher customer than helium. For carbon nuclei to fuse requires much hotter temperatures than a medium-sized star can generate—even in its fiery Red Giant phase.

So the Red Giant star, unable to fuse carbon for fuel, runs out of power. The tug of war that has gone on for billions of years between gravity and the star is over. Gravity wins. It collapses the Giant into a **WHITE DWARF**. This is a miniature star the size of the Earth. It's a dead star. It produces neither elements nor energy. Meanwhile the Giant's bright surface, the outside envelope of gas, floats away in a lovely nebula. (See photo in color photo section.)

Someday this will happen to our Sun. It will turn all of its fuel to carbon. There won't be enough heat to fuse carbon. The Sun's productive life will be over and gravity will scrunch it into a white dwarf.

THE REALLY BIG STARS

In a Giant's last days, nuclei in the center have fused from helium to carbon. At carbon is where most stars stop fusing.

Temperatures must be really hot to fuse carbon—hotter than 600 million degrees Kelvin. Most stars are not big enough to get that hot. Only a huge star with the gravity of its enormous mass pressing down on the center ever gets that hot.

When a *huge* star fuses carbon, it runs several different nuclear reactions at once. These reactions build up heavier and heavier atoms. The steps are so complicated that scientists still scratch their heads about some of them.

Carbon fusion in an enormous star may produce *nitrogen* (an atom with seven protons in its nucleus which gives it the atomic number of 7), *oxygen* (an atom with eight protons in its nucleus for an atomic number of 8), *fluorine* (nine protons, so #9) and the gas *neon* (#10 for 10 protons.)

Later steps can result in the light metals *sodium* (atomic #11), *magnesium* (atomic #12), and the heavy metal *aluminum* (#13.)

On the last day of its life, the swollen star may conjure *silicon* (#14), *phosphorous* (#15), *sulphur* (#16), *chlorine* (#17), the gas *argon* (#18), the light metals *potassium* (#19) and *calcium* (#20), and a rash of heavy metals including *scandium* (#21), *titanium* (#22), *vanadium* (#23), *chromium* (#24), *manganese* (#25), and finally, *iron* (#26)!

Phew! Busy day!

But not every atom is made inside the star. A few are made in collisions of nuclei on the surface or just outside the star.

In the end, *iron*, with 26 protons in its nucleus, is all that remains in the core of this very large star. There's something special about iron. Ever notice how strong something made of iron is? The nucleus of an iron atom is the most tightly bound up of all nuclei. This means it takes more energy to hold an iron atom together than any other atom.

STARBURST

Every once in a while in the universe, a really large star blows up. The explosion, called a **SUPERNOVA**, releases more energy in one second than our Sun will produce in its entire eight-billion-year lifetime. The blast of one supernova can shine more brightly than a galaxy with a billion stars.

When it's over, a supernova explosion may leave a dense nugget of a star about the size of New York City called a neutron star. Or it may leave a very hungry **BLACK HOLE**.

Supernova explosions only happen to the largest stars—those nine times larger than our Sun, at least. A star this large doesn't live very long, maybe a few million years. The more massive a star, the more pressure gravity puts on its center. So an enormous star fuses elements faster and reaches its Red Giant stage sooner than an ordinary star.

MORE ABOUT STARBURSTS

"When a star's center has fused all the way to iron, it stops fusing. A star just doesn't fuse anymore after that," said McDonald Observatory guide Bill Wren. "It takes more energy to fuse iron than iron creates when it is fused!"

Supernova 1987A.
**—University of Texas
Astronomy Department.**

*Supernova 1987A. The
way it appears today.*
**—University of Texas
Astronomy Department.**

63

By the time the core of a huge star has fused to iron, energy production has slowed to a stop. Now the star's old nemesis gravity closes in. Gravitational force crumples the outer shell of the star. The crumpling releases high energy gamma rays. Gamma rays shatter iron nuclei in the star's core. The iron core collapses.

It's a cosmic cave-in.

In less than a second, the star implodes and then explodes in a violent rebound. Nuclei falling toward the center jam up, like rush-hour traffic in Houston. The traffic backs up all the way to the star's surface. Material falling toward the center crashes into material blowing out from the center. The shock wave blasts the outer star into space.

A supernova is the most catastrophic blowout in nature. When it happens, atoms are splintered. Nuclei bind with other nuclei to create all kinds of new materials—66 new elements—heavier than iron!

Some of these new atoms you may have heard of, like the metals *cobalt* (atomic #27), *copper* (#29), *zinc* (#30), *silver* (#47), *platinum* (#78), *gold* (#79), and the poison *arsenic* (#33). Some, most of us have never heard of, like the metals *rubidium* (#37), *ruthenium* (#44), and *praseodymium* (#59). The ultimate product is *uranium*, with a nucleus filled by 92 protons and 146 neutrons.

Because these elements can only be made in a supernova, they are rare.

Add them to the elements that a large star manufactures prior to going supernova and you have 92—the total of elements found in nature. These elements and their combinations make up the physical universe, just like the letters of an alphabet make up a language.

INVAJION OF THE JEED PODJ

Supernovae not only produce elements heavier than iron. They also blast out all of the atoms that were locked in the star. The atoms drift about in space for millions of years until gravity presses them into a new star. The "new generation" star picks up where the star that exploded left off—churning with nuclear reactions, cooking nuclei into heavier nuclei.

LEAD INTO GOLD?

In medieval times, real-life wizards in the world's first laboratories toiled to turn ordinary metals, such as lead, into gold. This **PSEUDOSCIENCE**, known as **ALCHEMY**, was based on "magic." No matter how hard these **ALCHEMISTS** worked or how much they learned, they were never able to produce gold.

If they had known that it takes the most violent event we know of in the universe—a supernova—to do the job, they might have abandoned their labs forever. And chemistry might never have evolved into a science.

Our Sun got its heaviest elements from a star that blew up before it was born. And *that* star got its heavy atoms from a star that blew up before *it* was born.

So a supernova is like a bursting seed spore, sowing the universe with the atoms that new stars, planets, and people eventually are made from.

JUPERNOVA JECRETJ

On February 23, 1987, astronomer Ian Shelton saw a supernova explosion in the southern hemisphere sky. He saw it with his eyes, without a telescope. A star was blasting to smithereens in the Magellanic Cloud, a small galaxy that hangs close to the Milky Way.

Scientists say that within moments of our first view of the explosion, trillions of energy particles called **NEUTRINOS** hurtled from the supernova to Earth and zipped through our bodies. We didn't even notice! Today, astronomers still study Supernova 1987A. Its flash is still bright.

Supernovae have been spotted with the naked eye only a few times in recorded history. Most of the time they are seen with telescopes, in galaxies far from our own.

In fact, amateur astronomers using good telescopes discover up to 25 each year. Supernovae more distant than 75 million light years are hard to detect—except perhaps by radio telescopes, which are sensitive to invisible radio waves.

Scientists prefer star explosions that are closer by—ones that can be seen with optical telescopes. That's because theoreticians rely on spectroscopy to understand their dynamics. The best spectra are made of "nearby" explosions.

Supernovae are still a mystery to scientists in many ways. No one has been able to piece together a good computer model of one. Experts are still trying to figure them out. To find more supernovae to study, they rely on the observations of amateur night sky watchers around the world.

THE VIGIL

In the evenings when Bill Wren gets off work as a guide at the McDonald Observatory Visitors Center, he walks to a small building on a ridge on Mt. Locke where he keeps his specially designed telescope. He chooses clear nights to observe, when the moon is a thin crescent and won't fill the sky with light.

He makes himself comfortable in a chair and opens a ring binder containing hundreds of photos of different galaxies. For the next several hours, Wren compares these photos of galaxies with the actual galaxies he sees through his 18-inch reflector telescope.

He's looking for bright dots of light in the night sky that don't appear in the photographs. If he finds one, he may have a supernova.

To find more than one in a lifetime is a rare achievement shared by only a handful of amateur astronomers around the globe. Bill Wren has discovered two since he first began searching in 1990. The world record for spotting supernovae belongs to a minister in Australia, the Rev. Robert Evans, who has alerted astronomers to 26 previously unseen star explosions.

When Wren spotted his first supernova, it was about 5:00 in the morning. He was tired. He had already looked at 200 galaxies that night. The surprise patch of light appeared in a galaxy 70 million light years away, near the stars in the handle of the Big Dipper. Wren rubbed his eyes and looked again through the eyepiece. The light had not moved.

Wren filled out a form that amateur astronomers use when they think they've made a discovery. He sent the document over the computer to the Smithsonian Astronomical Observatory in Cambridge, Massachusetts. Then he dragged himself home to bed. It wasn't time to celebrate yet. Professional astronomers had to verify his find.

"Just because you see a new spot of light in a galaxy doesn't necessarily mean it's a supernova," Wren explained. "It could be an asteroid, or a previously unknown variable star in our own galaxy that has flared up. Or it could mean you misidentified the field and were looking at the wrong galaxy."

After 10 days, confirmation came from Asiago Observatory in Italy. Bill had judged right. He was the first person on the planet to spot this exploding star.

Two years passed. Early in the morning of August 17, 1994, Wren was using his 18-inch reflector telescope in his small building. Down the road, observatory superintendent Mark Adams and Marian Frueh, the observatory's resident astronomer, watched the sky on smaller telescopes.

Wren was observing "nearby" galaxies and comparing them with photographs when he paused to study galaxy NGC 5371, 50 million light years away. The galaxy showed a white spot that wasn't on his photograph.

He called Adams and Frueh away from their own stargazing. All three proceeded to study the new fleck of light in NGC 5371.

"After half an hour, we agreed that it was not moving. So I sent out my little telegram on the computer," Wren said.

This time confirmation came back in 20 hours. Astronomers at the University of California had scanned NGC 5371 just the week before. But their computerized telescope programmed to search "nearby" galaxies for starbursts had missed this one. After Wren's message, the California astronomers re-examined the recording and saw the smudge of light indicating that a star was just starting to blow up. The computer had not picked up on it.

McDonald Observatory as well as an observatory in Beijing, China, were put to work taking spectra of Wren's second supernova.

"It was a real exciting time," he said.

Interestingly, the supernova in NGC 5371 was in about the same part of the sky—near the Big Dipper's handle—as Wren's 1992 supernova.

"Now I know where to look," Wren joked.

Bill Wren has just finished building his own large "Supernovae Search Telescope," with a mirror arrangement that allows him to sit comfortably behind the eyepiece. A computerized motor rapidly moves the telescope from galaxy to galaxy. With this new device, Wren hopes to speed up his observations—from one galaxy per 70 seconds to one galaxy every 40 seconds. His goal is to check up to 500 galaxies on a single clear night. "My discovery rate should go up as a result," he said.

Wren's Supernova Search Telescope.
—Photo courtesy of Bill Wren and Dr. Craig Wheeler.

68

It took him between 20,000 and 30,000 observations of galaxies over the nights of six years to spot two supernovae. "I'm just getting started," he said excitedly.

As Wren finds them, astronomers who specialize in supernovae like Dr. Craig Wheeler at The University of Texas will investigate them with the largest spectroscopic telescope in the world, the Hobby Eberly Telescope.

4 SEEING THROUGH THE GATES

NIGHT ON THE MOUNTAIN

For most of the day, astronomers have slept in the TQ. Everyone has to be quiet here. Particularly in the daytime, residents are not allowed to talk in the hall. Residents may not speak above a whisper in their own rooms. Noise might wake the astronomers, who have stayed up all the previous night.

But there's no hushing the wind. For the past two days it has not stopped howling outside. All night long it whistled and wailed behind thick black window shutters in the room where we slept. The TQ sounded like a ship in a storm.

Today the gusts continue. Mountains around Mt. Locke float in a dusty haze.

At 5:00 P.M. astronomer David Lambert, a world expert on stars, pads from the dorm hall into the dining area. He pours himself a cup of coffee. Goldie Brown, the cook, offers to prepare him a full breakfast. He opts for milk and cornflakes instead.

Another astronomer joins him at the table. She is Suchitra Balachandra, a native of India working at Ohio State University. Goldie prepares her a vegetarian meal. Dr. Lambert and Dr. Balachandra have been up on Mt. Locke for two days, using the 107-inch telescope to study certain rare chemical elements being made inside older stars. Or they've been trying to. The wind has made it hard for the telescope to see well.

The astronomers are a little worried. Blowing sand and dust prevented observation until about 3:00 A.M. the night before. Every second counts at an observatory. Any part of the night not spent observing means precious time lost. Tonight may clear up. Balachandra and Lambert eat their meals without speaking to anyone.

The night before, when winds interrupted the astronomers'

work, Dr. Guillermo Gonzales was relaxed and talkative as he waited in the cafeteria for conditions to improve.

Tonight he keeps a low profile on the TQ's first floor. He slumps on an ottoman listening to the radio on earphones. He's being quiet because he doesn't want to wake any engineers who might be sleeping in the dorm.

Nobody's using the pool table. Although the room lights and TV are turned off, blinds are still drawn shut across the picture window. Dr. Gonzales closes his eyes and says little to us. He is disappointed because the dust is still flying outside on this second night and he can't look at the stars.

In the cafeteria, Mike Marcario, the astronomers' night assistant, chats with Victor Krabbendam, the engineer in charge of the primary mirror for the Hobby Eberly Telescope.

Two more astronomers suddenly enter the TQ, shutting freezing winds behind them. Having just arrived on the mountain, they head straight for the coffee pot. Dr. Inger Jorgensen of the McDonald Observatory staff in Austin and Dr. Arlin Crotts of New York's Columbia University look dressed for winter camping. What they'll really do up here is inspect galaxies 300 million light years away.

Dr. Jorgensen, who is Danish, explains that the distant galaxies she wants to look at are in the direction of the constellation Coma Berenices (which means Berenice's Hair).

"They're part of the nearest 'really big' cluster of galaxies, the Coma Cluster," she says. "Although 160 times farther away than the Andromeda Galaxy, the cluster is still considered part of the 'nearby' universe.

"Hundreds of galaxies are thought to be in the Coma Galaxy Cluster. But other galaxies in the same part of the sky may be closer, or more distant to us than the cluster. We'll be looking at emission lines to try to determine which galaxies in that direction are actually members of that cluster.

"The Coma Cluster is one of the well-studied clusters. But the knowledge of the fainter galaxies in it is fairly incomplete," Dr. Jorgensen says. She'll work with a multi-fiber instrument built by Dr. Crotts, who is here to help her use it. "It's really time consuming to observe the fainter galaxies. We'll set this fiber optic instrument designed by Arlan here on this field for an hour and get signals from

Hubble Deep Field
Hubble Space Telescope · WFPC2

The distant universe looks to be wall-to-wall galaxies, everywhere you look. In this famous Hubble Space Telescope photo of Deep Space, a couple of bright foreground stars belong to our Milky Way. All of the other flecks of light are remote galaxies.

—Robert Williams and the
Hubble Deep Field Team.
(STScI) NASA.

100 different galaxies fed into the spectrograph simultaneously. We may need four hours of integration time. But that is still much better than trying to get one galaxy at a time."

"Yeah, it works sometimes," Dr. Crotts says of his invention. He smiles.

"We'll be here six nights," Dr. Jorgensen continues. "It would be nice if, in that time, we looked at 600 galaxies. But if we get everything that I selected in those fields—that's about 400—then I would be very happy."

She puts both hands around her coffee mug to warm them.

"Even though we think we have studied the nearby universe in detail, this is not the case. The number counts on the faint galaxies in the nearby universe are actually very, very uncertain."

ON THE RADIO

The VLBA Radio Telescope below Mt. Locke.

—Mark G. Mitchell.

The radio telescope, a giant antenna dish, stands in a valley about five miles from Mt. Locke. It's a long, dusty, bouncy drive out there, on a narrow dirt road. Weighing 260 tons, the white dish rolls about on tiny wheels like a giant toy.

A high chain-link fence surrounds it and a trailer house next to it. The fence is posted with "Danger-Warning-High Voltage" signs.

John Holland, technician at the site, unlocks the gate for us. He opens the trailer's back door and ushers us into a work station crammed with computers spooling magnetic tape. Holland lives as well as works in this lonely outpost below Mt. Locke. He seems glad to have company.

Holland points out that he's not an astronomer but an electronics specialist. Astronomers in Soccoro, New Mexico, actually control the radio telescope.

The dish is part of a system of ten antennae called the Very Large Baseline Array (or VLBA) Radio Telescope. Stations operate in Texas, New Hampshire, Iowa, California, Washington, Hawaii, New Mexico, Arizona, and the Virgin Islands. Where one dish points, they all point. Together they create a radio receiver 5,000 miles wide.

The principle behind the VLBA is the bigger the receiver, the more astronomers can hear. Astronomers from around the world use the VLBA to pick up extremely faint radio emissions from objects in deep space.

"Astronomy here is very similar to what they do at McDonald Observatory—except we use a different part of the electromagnetic spectrum," Holland says. "In radio astronomy, we work with microwaves and millimeter waves.

"Optical astronomy uses a segment of the spectrum that for the most part is visible light. But visible light is just a small part of the electromagnetic spectrum. Any time an atom moves, you get a vibration. The vibration will be of a particular wavelength—between 0 frequency per second to 10 to the 24th power per second. All of these vibrations are the **ELECTROMAGNETIC SPECTRUM**.

"The spectrum also includes things we can hear. We can see the *visible* spectrum and we can hear the *audio* spectrum. These tiny parts of the spectrum are about all we're able to detect with our bodies. For everything else, we must build a machine to be able to receive it," Holland says.

"This dish looks at **MICROWAVES**, which are one form of radio waves. Telephone companies use microwaves to send long distance calls from one big tower to the next across the country. Those waves carry information just like the ones from space do."

Some radio telescopes search for possible signals from **EXTRA-**

TERREJTRIAL life. But the VLBA investigates the centers of galaxies and bright, high-energy sources at the far ends of the universe called **QUAJARJ**.

The VLBA also detects movements in the Earth's surface (like just before an earthquake). It does this by referencing the locations of the ten antennae with known stable things in space. It also registers small changes in the Earth's orbit.

Used together, the ten antennae dishes can perceive unusually fine detail in space. "Astronomers around the world like the VLBA. We've been producing **DATA** out here that's gone beyond their wildest dreams in terms of what they've been able to see," Holland says.

Any astronomer can submit a project for the dishes to examine, he adds. "You can send it over the Internet, and if it's approved—*boom!* You get your data processed. They correlate the tapes from the ten sites and put it on a little cartridge disc and send it to you and go on to whatever's next on the list."

TEXAJ' BIGGEJT JCIENCE PROJECT

The second largest "light bucket" in the world, the Hobby-Eberly Telescope (or HET), doesn't look or act like most telescopes. It uses 91 mirrors to make up the largest telescope mirror surface in North America.

It is a new breed of telescope called a spectroscopic survey telescope. It gathers photons from a celestial light source—a star, galaxy, comet, or distant planet—and feeds the light straight into a **JPECTROGRAPH**. The spectrograph spreads the light into an enormous spectrum, where astronomers see spectral absorption and emission lines with breathtaking precision.

Victor Krabbendam, the engineer in charge of building the primary mirror, explains, "The telescope rotates around on a turret but doesn't move up or down. It stays pointed at the same angle in the sky, about halfway between the horizon and the **ZENITH**."

A star moves across the surface of the mirrors for an hour or two, then goes out of range. The mirrors lay side by side in a tight honeycomb pattern. Each one can be adjusted by computer to make the best reflection of the star.

Marc Wetzel, observatory public information director, surveys the plate-shaped truss, or frame, that will support the Hobby Eberly Telescope's hexagonal mirrors.

—Mark G. Mitchell.

But stars appear to the HET as the Earth rotates. With this telescope, the big moving part is the Earth.

Through a round window in the HET's dome (resembling a window in a birdhouse), the 91 mirrors watch the sky. "Picture the sky moving past," says McDonald Observatory Director Dr. Frank Bash. "There's a star you want to look at. The star's light comes down and hits the mirror and reflects off to a point up here . . ." He cups his hand upside-down above an imaginary telescope. Here, where Dr. Bash holds his cupped hand, engineers have installed a detector. The detector gathers up reflected light in the same way that a bee gathers pollen.

"As that star apparently moves across the sky this way, the star's reflection moves the opposite way," Bash says. Attached to a moving instrument, the detector tracks the reflection as it moves across the surface of the mirrors. An instrument on the tracker sends light signals to one of several spectrographs in a control room, off the side of the telescope. The light is analyzed.

"If the telescope needs to see more of the star later in the night," Krabbendam says, "the mirror can be pivoted around and catch the star on its descent back to the horizon. It can track it for another hour or two, until the star arcs out of view again."

The HET looks at the spectra—the rainbows—of stars and galaxies in detail that has never been seen before. "It puts us in the forefront of astronomical research," Dr. Bash says.

It is also changing life a bit at the observatory.

Astronomers don't have to travel to the Davis Mountains to work with the telescope. Instead, they send their assignments in. A computer arranges the observations.

The HET is owned by several partners who use it: The University of Texas, Pennsylvania State University, Stanford University, and two German universities, the Ludwig-Maximilians-Universitat Munchen and Georg-August-Universitat Gottingen.

"The first object the telescope sees in a night may be for Penn State astronomers," Bash says. "The next object may be for the Stanford astronomers. The third and the fourth may be for Texas.

The Hobby Eberly Telescope (HET) under construction in 1996. The geodesic dome top lies on the ground beside the building.
—Thomas A. Sebring, Hobby Eberly Telescope Project.

The computer makes up the nightly schedules depending on the night's weather, the importance of the objects, and all kinds of factors.

"This changes the culture at the observatory because the astronomers stay home and the data is sent to them over the Internet the morning after it is taken. We're accustomed to going out there, sleeping in the daytime and working all night. So this really means a change for all of us," Dr. Bash says.

Although the HET's mirror is the largest in the world, it can't see an especially big view of the sky. It sees a patch of sky only about one-tenth the diameter of the Moon. The Harlan J. Smith 107-inch telescope, which was built to take wide field photographs, can see a piece of sky as wide as two full moons, side by side.

Although the HET's vision is narrow, its view is profound. It looks far and deep, registering objects that are extremely small and faint, like the planets of other stars, or the most distant objects known, **QUAJARJ**.

The HET can see all the way back in time to the edge of our universe—to within only years of the Big Bang. John McDonald, the man who dreamed of the observatory, would have approved.

UP IN THE DOME

The Sun drops between Sawtooth Mountain and Mount Livermore, in the direction of El Paso. The wind has stopped.

Almost everyone who works in the beehive of the large dome has gone home for the day, but Dr. Lambert and Dr. Balachandra are just reporting for work. We follow them into an elevator.

When the elevator reaches the dome's fifth floor, lights in the compartment shut off by themselves. We wait in pitch blackness until the doors roll open. We enter a sort of gymnasium in which the Harlan J. Smith 107-inch telescope looms like a colossal X-ray machine.

The astronomers climb steps to a room located off to one side of the telescope. They open a door to an insulated space, a separate control room, lit by a desk lamp and two glowing computer screens.

Out on the main floor, Mike Marcario, the night assistant, is already on duty on the telescope platform. His only light comes from the open shutter in the dome. As dusk falls, he punches a button on an instrument panel. And with the loud *chakunk* of the hydraulic release, the platform rises, bringing Mike close to the telescope eyepiece. He checks the temperature of a brass cylinder that bathes the CCD in liquid nitrogen to keep it freezing cold. The slightest heat overwhelms the CCD's signal.

On a computer on the platform, Mike keys in the coordinates of the stars Dr. Lambert and Dr. Balachandra have selected for observation for the night. He punches another button and the dome ceiling stirs to life. Metal groans against metal. The floor rumbles. Bearings squeal and jangle as the giant dome rotates in its tracks. The echoes of these sounds chase each other around and around the room. Watching, we feel that we're the ones whirling while the dome is standing still. We're dizzy until the motion stops.

Mike pushes another button. The dome shutter doors open with a moan, revealing a large rectangle of pure sky, neither light nor dark—a magic window.

Mike pushes another button and the telescope rolls up on its axle with the majesty of a rising whale. A repeating, high-pitched *beep* warns us to look out for the swinging, 160-ton assembly.

Dr. David Lambert wears a worn cotton flannel shirt, baggy khaki pants, and hiking shoes. He got his Ph.D. studying the Sun. He speaks in the accent of his native Great Britain, where he worked as an astronomer at Oxford University before coming to The University of Texas.

He and Dr. Balachandra sit facing two old computers. They use an intercom to talk with Mike. He's just outside their enclosure, where the telescope now points at a high angle to a single star. They are anxious to start work for the night, but Dr. Lambert has set aside a few moments to talk. He tells us why he studies the stars.

"One of the biggest questions in science is probably related to the origins of the chemical elements. Apart from hydrogen and helium, and ignoring one or two little details, all of the chemical elements that make life possible have been made inside stars," he says.

"By studying stars—how they evolve, how they live and die—we're hoping not only to understand them as individuals, but we're trying to understand what drives their evolution, what makes them big, what makes them small. We're also trying to understand the role they play in making all of the chemical elements."

"You can't get a much bigger question than that," he says.

This week, Dr. Lambert explains, they've been trying to find an element in stars called beryllium.

"There's not much beryllium anywhere. That's because of the way it's made. It's not made in stars. *It's one of the exceptions*," he says.

Scientists believe that beryllium is actually made in the gas *between* stars. Dr. Lambert explains, "At very high energies, particles—mostly hydrogen nuclei and helium nuclei—go whizzing through the gas, and every now and then they hit an oxygen atom or the nucleus of an oxygen atom and chip a bit off. And some of these bits are beryllium.

"It's not a very efficient process because there aren't that many high energy particles. Beryllium is also a very fragile element. When it gets inside a star, it is very easily destroyed.

"So we're looking at a group of stars, some of which have destroyed another element, lithium, which is even more fragile than beryllium. And we're trying to see if those stars that have destroyed lithium, have destroyed beryllium as well.

"If the hot inside of the star is mixing up quite a bit with the star's cooler surface, beryllium is probably being destroyed along with lithium. If the mixing between the core and the surface is more shallow, only the more fragile element, lithium, is being destroyed."

They plan to spend the first half of the night looking at just one star—ARCTURUS. They'll spend the second half pointing the telescope to different bright stars all over the sky. So they are aiming the telescope at a pinpoint of light in space, trying to detect fragile beryllium atoms on the light's surface. To help them, they're relying on the world's largest spectrograph downstairs.

"The problem is that the spectral lines that we use to detect beryllium are in the ultraviolet end of the spectrum and the atmosphere isn't very transparent at that wavelength," Dr. Lambert says. "Nor is our equipment very sensitive at that wavelength. So it is a bit of a struggle to detect these lines." He gives us an urgent look.

To make matters worse, viewing has been poor all week.

"The atmosphere has been very turbulent. Wind and dust have got in the way. The atmosphere bends light, and air of different temperatures and different densities bends light differently.

LAST LIGHT

To the ancient Greeks, Arcturus was part of the constellation Bootes (BOO-tiss). The name referred to an old herdsman who watched over his cattle every night in the heavens.

Navajos in New Mexico had a different name for Arcturus. They called this star the Coyote's Eyeball.

According to legend, a young male coyote was trying to show off in front of a group of female coyotes. He took his eyeballs out of his face, tossed them up in the air, and started doing fancy tricks with them. He flung one eyeball under his leg and the other over his head. He juggled them behind his back. He juggled them high into the sky—until one eyeball stuck and never fell back. The female coyotes were not impressed. The coyote had only one eye after that. But the night had gained its third brightest star.

Another fabulous story to add to the Arcturus lore: Arcturus is a cool Red Giant star 20 times larger than our Sun. It lies 36 light years or 212 trillion (212,000,000,000,000) miles from our solar system. And tonight astronomers were reading messages from the atoms in its fires.

"So if you have a blob of warm air over here and a blob of cold air over here and the parallel light from the star is going through those blobs, the light wave at the left may come out at this angle and the light wave on the right may come out at a different angle.

81

So the poor old telescope, which wants to take parallel light and focus it to a point, doesn't collect parallel light. It gets a beam in which the rays of light are pointing in a variety of directions. And so it can't produce a point. It produces some blurry patch. And the blobs of air are moving with the wind so that the patch is jumping all over the place."

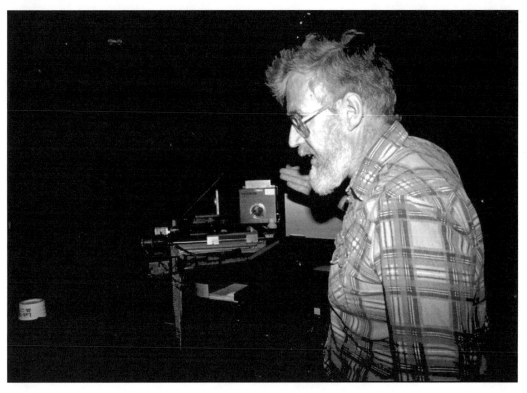

Dr. David Lambert in the Spectrograph Room.
—Mark G. Mitchell.

The spectrograph downstairs contains an eyepiece with a tiny hair-line slit that astronomers want starlight to go through.

"Last night the star image [from the telescope] was much bigger than the slit and moving all over the place," Dr. Lambert says. "Tonight hopefully the star image will be small, and much more of the light will go through into the detector."

They take us down to the Coude Spectrograph Room on the floor just below the dome's top floor. Not everyone gets to come here. We're trespassing on astronomers' sacred ground.

The Spectrograph Room would be a great place for a Halloween party. It's like a dungeon, with a spooky low ceiling and coal-black walls. Two giant piers on either side of us drop all the way to bedrock to support the great telescope upstairs. The piers are painted dull black—just like the walls and the steel grating under our feet. The black is to stop stray light from being reflected around.

Dr. Lambert switches on a lonely light to reveal a flea market for physicists—tables and benches piled with old-fashioned looking scientific equipment: tubes, mirrors, metal plates, metal boxes, gizmos, cameras, cables, and wires.

We're looking at the largest spectrograph assembly—in terms of sheer space occupied—in the world. The items on the benches and tables, we learn, are passageways for beams of light.

Upstairs, light is collected from the primary telescope mirror. The light travels through a series of tubes that look like large utility pipes. Mirrors in these tubes bounce the light down here to the Coude Spectrograph.

"Most people think it's Monsieur Coude who invented something or other. But actually *coude* is a French word meaning 'elbow'," Lambert says. "The name is simply appropriate because the light path has got a bend in it. This one has two bends in it to get down to where we look at it."

He leads us through the maze of dark, bulky equipment.

"The light travels down here. This mirror makes the light parallel, and directs it to this thing we call the **GRATING**." He shows us a pane of frosted window glass. The grating consists of a piece of glass in which there are very fine rulings cut, which spread the light out into the different colors.

The light, by the time it reaches Dr. Lambert's electronic camera, has traveled 200 feet from the telescope's mirror. Such distances are good for spectrography. The farther you can coax light to wander through your contraption, the wider you can spread it out. That's the best way to see its thousands of wavelengths.

We're back in the fifth-floor control room now. It's almost 9:00 P.M. and you can tell the astronomers are itching to get to work.

"Through the night we'll be monitoring what comes back, what we collect. We'll look at the spectra and see if it's of high enough quality—whether we need to take a second exposure or a third. Or whether the exposure is so low in quality we need to move to a brighter object—a different star.

"Some nights one makes exciting discoveries in real time. Here we're going to take the data away and work on it. With the particular program we're using, it's a bit hard to realize you've got a striking discovery.

"Most of these stars are probably going to have beryllium. The interest is *how much*. The quantitative answer you can't get from the computer screen. You've got to take it away and work on it."

The stars are coming out. It is time to start observing. We wish them luck and leave them to their work in the dome.

Twilight has turned to night. The familiar landmarks of the main floor have disappeared. Shadow hides the great disc of the 107-inch mirror, the raised platform and even Mike, the night assistant. All we can see are the glowing red numbers on Mike's instruments and the telescope's bold form against a twinkling night sky—a sky that holds the mysteries of the universe.

MORE ABOUT THE McDONALD OBSERVATORY

At the McDonald Observatory Visitors' Center. Viewing 17,000 mile-high flare-ups on the sun's surface.
—Mark G. Mitchell.

You can visit McDonald Observatory. Located on two mountain tops off Highway 118 about 17 miles north of Fort Davis, Texas, the observatory is one of the state's most popular and scenic tourism spots, as well as the highest location in Texas reachable by road.

Guided public tours begin at the summit of Mt. Locke at 2:00 P.M., seven days a week, except Thanksgiving, Christmas, and New Year's Day. Cost is $2 for adults, $1 for children. The tour includes a trip into the large dome to see the 107-inch Harlan J. Smith telescope. Self-guided tours are also possible during business hours. You can walk into the dome by yourself to see the 107-inch telescope. But you must climb five flights of stairs. For the guided group tours, a freight elevator is available for a ride to the telescope floor.

On Mt. Fowlkes, the George T. Abell Visitors Gallery allows visitors to learn about research astronomy and see the Hobby Eberly Telescope at close range through a glass enclosure.

At the base of Mt. Locke on Highway 118, the W.L. Moody Visitors Center features exhibits, books, starcharts, posters, merchandise, and

85

educational toys. The center also shows videos about the observatory. Hours are 9:00 to 5:00 daily. Telescope viewings of the sun are 11:00 A.M. and 3:30 P.M. daily. Star parties begin 30 minutes after sunset on Tuesday, Friday, and Saturday nights, weather permitting.

For more information call (915) 426-3640 or consult the McDonald Observatory website at http://pio.as.utexas.edu.

TEXAS PLANETARIUMS

Great skies for star-gazing bless Texas, as do many planetariums, museums, and science centers—not to mention NASA's Johnson Space Center in Houston. Planetariums present programs ranging from "Why did the dinosaurs die?" to "Backyard astronomy." Here are the ones open to the public.

ABILENE

Morgan Jones Planetarium, operated by the Abilene School District, on 700 North Mockingbird, presents public shows two or three evenings a year that are advertised locally. (915) 677-1444

AMARILLO

Don Harrington Discovery Center on 1200 Street Drive. The planetarium features educational star shows and laser rock concerts. Prices range from $2 to $5 depending on the event. Call (806) 355-9547 for hours and programs.

ARLINGTON

The University of Texas-Arlington Planetarium presents public shows every first Friday of the month from 8:00 to 9:00 P.M., with certain holiday exceptions. Available for hire for specialized shows for groups. For more information call Dr. Ulrich O. Herrmann or Dr. James Gelb (817) 273-2266.

AUSTIN

Austin Nature Center, Zilker Park. Call (512) 327-8180 for times and dates of tent planetarium shows.

University of Texas Skywatcher Report—Call (512) 471-5007 for night sky reports recorded weekly. At the university's old Painter Hall Observatory, telescope viewing is scheduled every clear Saturday night

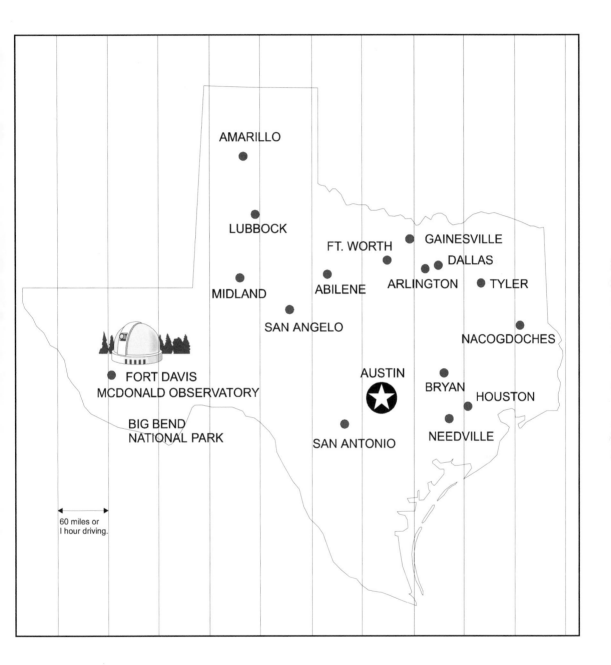

LOCATIONS OF TEXAS PLANETARIUMS

after dark. Public Star Parties are held Wednesday nights on the roof (14 floors up) of Robert Lee Moore Hall, 26th and Speedway. (512) 471-1307

Wild Basin Wilderness Preserve, one mile north of the intersection of Bee Caves Road and Loop 360 (Capital of Texas Highway), presents stargazing and moonlight tours each month. $2 adults. (512) 327-7622

BRYAN-COLLEGE STATION
Texas A&M Observatory offers public night sky viewing. For details call the observatory after dark at (409) 845-0536.

DALLAS
The Science Place Planetarium, Southwest Museum of Science and Technology, 1318 Second Avenue, offers programs marking astronomical events such as eclipses and comets. Shows every hour and a half during the Texas State Fair season. Special programs can be scheduled for groups. In the summer the planetarium conducts general astronomy classes for children and a star party/safari to a local wildlife ranch. Open 9:30 A.M. to 5:30 P.M. Monday through Saturday; noon to 5:30 P.M. Sunday. Admission is $3 per person. Visitors also can buy combination tickets that include the museum ($7 adults, $5.50 children and senior citizens). Group tours are scheduled through the scheduling coordinator at (214) 428-5555.

St. Mark's Planetarium and Observatory, at St. Mark's School, 10600 Preston Road, offers no public shows. But arrangements can be made for special group shows (seats 80). Call Stephen Balog, science teacher at (214) 363-6491, ext 166.

Richland College Planetarium, Sabine Hall, RM SS161, 2800 Abrams Road, presents public educational programs by the Texas Astronomical Society (example, "Footsteps—Man's Fascination with the Moon") Saturday afterrnoons at 2:00 P.M. and 3:00 P.M. with a live star show and telescope viewing some evenings. Admission is free, donations accepted. (214) 238-6013

EL PASO
El Paso Planetarium, 6531 Boeing Drive, operated by El Paso ISD, presents public programs (example, "Comets Are Coming"). Call (915) 779-4400 for dates and programs. Admission $2 per person. Also operates a recorded Star Line after 5:00 P.M. (915) 779-4317 discussing what's in the sky each month.

FORT WORTH
Noble Planetarium, Fort Worth Museum of Science and History, 1501

Montgomery Street, presents public shows Wednesday, Thursday and Friday every half hour between 2:30 and 4:30 P.M., Saturday between 11:00 A.M. and 4:30 P.M. every half hour, and Sunday between 12:30 and 4:30 every half hour (example, "Hubblevision, Six Years of Amazing Telescope Images"). Shows are $3, all ages. (817) 732-1631

GAINESVILLE
North Central Texas College Planetarium at 1525 W. California, presents public shows at different times of the year. (817) 668-7731

HOUSTON
Burke Baker Planetarium, Houston Museum of Natural Science, 1 Hermann Circle Drive, presents shows daily at 3:00, Saturdays and Sundays at 11:00, 1:00, and 3:00 P.M. (examples, "Case of the Disappearing Dinosaurs," "Stargazers Guide," "Symphony to the Stars") $3 nonmember adults, $2 for senior citizens and children age 3-11. (713) 639-4629

NASA-Johnson Space Center, 2101 NASA Road 1. Operated by the U.S. government. Open 10:00 A.M. to 7:00 P.M. on weekends, 10:00 A.M. to 5:00 P.M. during the week. 40 hands-on exhibits for children, starship gallery, small planetarium. Plan to spend five and a half hours to see everything, including the tram tours to NASA where the astronauts train, and Rocket Park. Admission $11.95 adults, $8.50 children age 4-11 ($3 parking fee). Bring your camera. For information call (800) 972-0369. (Traveling on 45 South, take NASA exit 25, go east three miles, watch for a spaceman behind the golden arches of McDonald's Restaurant on the left. NASA is the next light on the left.)

LUBBOCK
Moody Planetarium, Texas Tech University, Fourth and Indiana, has shows Thursday at 7:30 P.M., Tuesday through Friday at 3:30 P.M., and Sunday at 2:00 and 3:30. $1 adults, 50 cents students, including university students. Adults over 60 and children under 5 are free. (806) 742-2432

MIDLAND/ODESSA
Marian Blakemore Planetarium, Museum of the Southwest, 1705 W. Missouri, features public shows on the *first weekend* of every month (Saturday and Sunday) with a children's show (example, "Space Bus") at 11:00 P.M. and adult show ("West Texas Skies") at 8:00 P.M. Friday and 1:00 P.M. Saturday. Admission $2 adults, $1 children. (916) 683-2882

NACOGDOCHES
Stephen F. Austin State University Planetarium, Physics and Astronomy Dept., features public shows Sundays at 2:30 and 4:00 P.M.

and Tuesdays at 7:30 P.M. with programs that change every 6-8 weeks (examples "Mars," "Comets"). Admission $2 adults, $1.50 children. For information, (409) 468-3001. Call (409) 468-3009 for a recorded message and an episode of the radio program *Stardate*.

NEEDVILLE
George Observatory at Brazos Bend State Park, Needville, Texas, has a 36-inch telescope for public viewing. (713) 242-3055

SAN ANGELO
Angelo State University Planetarium, Nursing and Physical Science Center, Vanderventer Street presents public shows at 8:00 P.M. Thursdays and 2:00 P.M. Saturdays (example, "Through the Eyes of Hubble"). Admission: adults $3, students and senior citizens $1.50. (915) 942-2136

SAN ANTONIO
Scobee Planetarium, 1300 San Pedro Avenue, operated by San Antonio College Continuing Education and Outreach Division, presents a children's show at 6:30 P.M. and a general audience program at 8:00 P.M. every Friday. Programs for schools (kindergarten through high school) Monday through Thursday by appointment. Admission currently free. (210) 733-2910

TYLER
Hudnall Planetarium, Tyler Junior College, Lake Street, presents shows Wednesday at 1:00 P.M. and Sunday at 2:00 P.M. except for holidays, (example, "More than meets the eye: What you can see when you look through a small telescope). $1.50 adults, $1 children age 4-11 and adults over 60. Monthly star parties and summer children's classes. Also group reservations for special shows can be made. (903) 510-2312

ASTRONOMICAL WORDS

Absorb (Absorption): To take in, receive, or soak up.

Absorption spectrum: A spectrum of dark (absorption) lines. These lines are actually gaps in the spectrum where photons have been absorbed.

Alchemists: Persons who practiced alchemy, or tried to turn lead into gold.

Alchemy: A medieval philosophy that common metals could be turned into gold.

Angstrom: A tiny unit for measuring wavelengths of light. One angstrom is one ten billionth of a meter.

Arcturus: At 36 light years away, Arcturus is one of the closest bright stars to the earth. Follow the arc of the handle of the Big Dipper—it is the first bright star you come to out in the sky.

Asteroid: A piece of a planet that never formed and orbits the sun. (Asteroids are 600 miles in diameter or less.)

Astronomers: Scientists who are skilled in astronomy or the observation of objects and phenomena beyond the earth.

Astronomy: The science of outer space, including the study of the chemistry, sizes, and motions of objects in space.

Atom: The smallest possible unit of a chemical element. It consists of a nucleus (protons and neutrons) and one or more orbiting electrons.

Axis: An imaginary straight line through the center of a planet around which the planet rotates.

Big Bang: An explosion of matter and energy that many scientists believe created the universe.

Binary stars: Two stars that orbit each other around a common center of gravity.

Black Hole: A giant star that has collapsed to a pinpoint. Gravitational pull of this point is so strong that no radiation can escape from it.

Blue-shifted: Wavelengths shortened as the source of light and the observer approached each other.

Carbon-nitrogen-oxygen cycle: A series of nuclear reactions common in a star more massive than our Sun. In a process that uses carbon in the star's core, helium atoms are fused from hydrogen atoms.

Catastrophic: Disastrous or happening with a violent overturn.

CCD (Charge Coupled Device): A small, wafer-shaped electronic device with thousands of light-sensitive elements to record very faint images in space.

Celestial mechanics: Study of the movements in space of planets, moons, asteroids, and comets.

Convection: The transfer of heat in a fluid by motions in the fluid.

91

Data: Fact-based information used for reasoning or calculating.

Destabilize: To upset or make unstable.

Doppler Effect: A change in wavelength that occurs when the source of the waves moves toward or away from an observer.

Electromagnetic radiation: Changing electric and magnetic fields that travel through space, carrying energy.

Electromagnetic spectrum: The full range of wavelengths of radiation, from gamma rays to the longest radio waves.

Electron: A tiny spark-like particle that orbits an atom's nucleus. It carries a negative electrical charge and contains only 1/1830th the mass of a proton.

Element: An atom characterized by a certain number of protons in its nucleus. Atoms of a given element all have the same chemical properties.

Emission spectrum: (Sometimes called a "Bright Line Spectrum") A spectrum of bright lines caused by the emission of photons from atoms.

Emit (Emission): To release, give off, or send out.

Extraterrestrial: Originating from beyond earth.

Fusion: The creation of heavier nuclei from lighter nuclei, resulting in the release of enormous energy.

Galaxy: One of billions of systems of stars and nebulae that make up the universe.

Gamma ray: An intense electromagnetic radiation with wavelengths shorter than one angstrom.

Grating: (in astronomy) A sheet of glass, plexiglass, or celluloid with thousands of lines etched in it. The lines bend lightwaves to produce a spectrum.

Gravity: The attraction that one great mass in space, like a moon or a planet, has for another mass.

Greenhouse Effect: The trapping of heat on Earth by the atmosphere.

Heavy hydrogen: A hydrogen atom consisting of a proton, a neutron, and an electron. Light hydrogen does not have a neutron.

Infrared: Electromagnetic radiation with wavelengths longer than red light's 7000 angstroms—and shorter than one millimeter.

Isotopes: Atoms that have the same number of protons but a different number of neutrons. You can think of them as different "versions" of an element. For example, Carbon 12 is a carbon atom with six protons (which carbon *must* have) and six neutrons. But other forms of carbon can have seven or eight neutrons.

Light year: A unit of measurement astronomers use to measure great distances in space. It is the distance light travels in one year—about 5.9 trillion miles.

Luminosity: How much light is emitted by a light source.

Mass: A measure of how much matter an object contains.

Microwave: Electromagnetic radiation with wavelengths that range between one centimeter and one meter.

Milky Way: Name given to our galaxy.

Molecules: Two or more atoms bonded together.

Multiple Star Systems: Two or more stars that orbit each other or a common center of mass.

Nebulae: An immense cloud of gas and dust in space.

Neutrino: A weightless atomic particle that travels at the speed of light.

Neutron: An atomic particle in the nucleus of all atoms except light hydrogen. A neutron is about the same mass as a proton, but carries no electrical charge.

Nucleus: The core of an atom, containing protons and neutrons. Each proton has a positive electrical charge.

Orange Giant Star: A swollen star in the later stages of life. It is cooler than our Sun, but not as cool as a Red Giant.

Photon: A quantun (or particle) of radiant energy or light.

Photosynthesis: The process used by plants to make food from sunlight.

Pixels: Detectors on a CCD or a microchip on a video camera. Pixels translate photons into an electronic charge so an image can be stored. Pixel is short for "Picture Element."

Primary mirror: The main mirror in a reflector telescope. It collects light from the sky.

Prism: A transparent (glass) shape with two of its sides nonparallel. A prism bends light, separating its wavelengths.

Pristine: Remaining pure or original.

Proton: A positive-charged particle in the nucleus of an atom.

Proton-proton chain: The simplest nuclear reaction in the core of a star that produces helium from hydrogen. Four hydrogen nuclei combine in step-by-step sequence to form a nucleus of helium. The process releases energy and makes the stars shine.

Proxima Centauri: A tiny red dwarf star about 4.2 light years away in the constellation Centaur, which is not visible in our hemisphere.

Pseudoscience: A system of beliefs, theories, and methods that may seem scientific but really isn't.

Pulsate: To throb, pulse, or move in a steady rhythm.

Quasars: Derived from two words—quasi-stellar. These are small, powerful energy sources in deep space. Scientists think they may be the hearts of distant galaxies.

Red Giant Star: A star that has become larger and cooler in the late stages of its life. A Red Giant is 10 to 100 times larger than our Sun.

Red shift: The shift of spectral absorption or emission lines to the longer wavelength end of the spectrum.

Reflector telescope: A telescope that uses a mirror to form the observed image.

Satellite: A body that orbits a larger body in space, such as a moon that orbits a planet.

Spectrum (Spectra): Electromagnetic radiation spread out by wavelength.

Spectrograph: A device that separates light into its wavelengths in perfect order from the shortest to the longest. A spectroscope with a camera.

Spectroscope: An instrument that allows chemists and astronomers to resolve or observe spectra.

Supernova (Supernovae): The explosion of a star at least nine times more massive than our Sun. It happens at the end of the star's life, when gravity crumples it into a neutron star or a black hole, releasing incredible amounts of energy and radiation.

Trajectory: The curved path that a body (a planet, a comet, or a rocket) travels in space.

Transient Quarters ("TQ"): Dormitory built on a cliff atop Mt. Locke at McDonald Observatory, where astronomers stay.

Ultraviolet rays: Electromagnetic radiation with wavelengths between 100 and 4000 angstroms.

Variable star: A star with a pattern of changing brightness.

Visible light: Light or electromagnetic radiation that human eyes can see.

Wavelength: The distance of one oscillation or vibration in a wave.

White Dwarf: A star that gravity has collapsed to about the size of our Earth. It's the last stage for stars smaller than one and a half times our Sun.

X-Rays: Electromagnetic radiation with wavelengths between 1 and 100 angstroms.

Zenith: Highest point in the sky.

KNOW YOUR UNIVERSE

My written sources included the McDonald Observatory files at the Center for American Studies at The University of Texas, Austin, and the following:

Alchemy of the Heavens: Searching for Meaning in the Milky Way by Ken Croswell. New York: Anchor Books. Bantam Doubleday, Dell, 1995.

Big and Bright: A History of the McDonald Observatory by David Evans and J. Derral Mulholland. Austin: University of Texas Press, 1986.

The Supernova Story by Laurence A. Marschall. New York: Plenum Press, 1988.

Contemporary Astronomy by Jay M. Pasachoff. Saunders College Publishing, 1985.

Foundations of Astronomy by Michael Seeds. Wadsworth Publishing Company, 1994.

Earth, Moon and Stars, More Than Magnifiers and Oobleck. GEMS (Great Explorations in Math & Science) Guides, Lawrence Hall of Science, University of California at Berkeley.

Here are some resources you might enjoy:

Adler, Irving. *The Stars: Decoding Their Messages.* New York: Thomas Y. Crowell, 1956, revised 1980.

Bradley, Franklyn. *Sun Dogs and Shooting Stars: A Skywatcher's Guide.* New York: Avon Books, 1993.

Darling, Dr. David. *Could You Ever Build a Time Machine?* Minneapolis, Minnesota: Dillon Press, Inc., 1991.

Dickinson, Terence. *Exploring the Night Sky.* Buffalo, New York: Camden House Publishing, Ontario: Firefly Books, 1987.

Dolan, Terrance. *Deep Space* (World Explorers Series). New York: Chelsea Publishers, 1993.

Gallant, Roy A. *Private Lives of the Stars.* New York: Macmillan Publishing Company, 1986.

Kondo, Herbert. *Adventures in Space and Time: The Story of Relativity.* New York: Holiday House, 1966.

Levy, David H., consulting editor. *Stars and Planets.* Time Life Books (The Nature Company Discoveries Library), 1996.

——. *Skywatching.* Time Life Books (The Nature Company Guides), 1995.

McAleer, Neil. *The Cosmic Mind-Boggling Book.* With a foreword by Robert Jastrow. Warner Books, 1982.

Pasachoff, Jay M., and Donald H. Menzel. *Discovering Stars and Planets.* Peterson Field Guides. Boston: Houghton Mifflin Company, 1992.

Simon, Seymour. *The Long View into Space.* New York: Crown Publishers, Inc., 1979.

Magazines:
Astronomy
Odyssey
Sky and Telescope
Stardate, published bimonthly by the McDonald Observatory Public Information Office, (1-800-782-7328)

Radio programs:
Earth and Sky
Stardate

Websites:
Earth and Sky
http.//www.earthsky.com

Jet Propulsion Laboratory Planetary Image Archive (PIA):
http://www-pdsimage.jpl.nasa.gov/PIA
http:/www.jpl.nasa.gov/releases/imagesvv.html
http:/newproducts.jpl.nasa.gov/comet
http://encke.jpl.nasa.gov.

McDonald Observatory
http://pio.as.utexas.edu.

NASA Mission to Planet Earth Home Page
http://www.hq.nasa.gov/office/mtpe

National Optical Astronomical Observatory
http://www/noao.edu

The Planetary Society
http://planetary.org/tps/

NASA SpaceLink
http://spacelink.msfc.nasa.gov

NEAR (Near Earth Asteroid Rendezvous) Mission
http://hurlbut.juapl.edu/NEAR/intro

Space Science Education Home Page
http://www/gsfc.nasa.gov/education/education_home.html

Space Telescope Science Institute (Hubble)
http:// www.stsci.edu/pubinfo/pictures.html

Stardate
http://www.stardate.utexas.edu

Stardate Guide to Solar System
http://www.as.utexas.edu/McDonald/VC/Education/S.S.Guide

U.S. Geological Survey
http://pdsimage.wr.usgs.gov/PIA

ACKNOWLEDGMENTS

This book owes its existence to the City of Austin, the Austin Arts Commission, the Austin Writer's League, and corporate sponsors, Texas Crushed Stone Corporation and Wenzel Associates, Inc.

I relied on the help, inspiration, and eloquence of many people to create *Seeing Stars*. My heartfelt thanks to Dr. Chris Sneden, who served as reporting source as well as consulting editor; Marsha Mitchell, my partner in life and in reporting for this book; my mother Alice Mitchell, who reviewed the clunky first draft and liked it; Scott Mitchell, my brother and the former president of the Houston Astronomical Society, who assisted throughout the research and writing; and publishers Ed Eakin and Virginia Messer and editor Melissa Roberts of Eakin Press for their support and usual good guidance.

My deepest appreciation extends to the McDonald Observatory director, Dr. Frank Bash, for his help and his gracious preface.

And to the following people whose kind cooperation will always be remembered by me: astronomers Dr. Kay Hemenway; Dr. Inger Jorgenson; Dr. David Lambert; Dr. Art Whipple and Dr. Guillermo Gonzales of The University of Texas; Dr. Arlan Crotts, Columbia University; Dr. Suchitra Balachandra, formerly of Ohio State University; the Supernovae Spotting Project team of Bill Wren and Dr. J. Craig Wheeler; and the Hobby Eberly Telescope crew of Tom Sebring, Victor Krabbendam, and Annamaria Sergi.

McDonald Observatory staffers Marc Wetzel; Ed Dutchover; Earl Green; John Holland; Goldie Brown; Mike Marcario; Jane Wiant.

At *Stardate* magazine: Tim Jones, production artist; Sandra Barnes, business manager; Susanne Harm, circulation manager.

Also at The University of Texas: Joyce Samson; Anil Dosaj; Molly Wright; Laura Eakins; and Caroline Compton.

And outside UT's walls: Jane Runnels, Ph.D., Brian Yamada; Cheryl Kempf; Angela Smith (executive director) and Sally Baker (associate director) of the Austin Writer's League; Tim Taylor (Holt-Rhinehart Publishers); Mike Gentry (Media Affairs, NASA, Johnson Space Center); writers Tamra Andrews and Jeff Kanipe.

And special thanks to David Levy.

INDEX

ABOUT THE AUTHOR

Mark G. Mitchell watches stars from his driveway in Austin, Texas. His writing credits range from the children's magazine *Cricket,* to *American Artist's Watercolor* (where he is a contributing editor), to the internationally broadcasted radio series *Earth and Sky.* He is the author-illustrator of *The Mustang Professor* (Eakin Press), which *Review of Texas Books* called "a must for all public and school libraries," and has illustrated numerous children's books.

ABOUT THE CONSULTING EDITOR

Christopher Sneden, **Ph.D.,** is professor of astronomy at The University of Texas-Austin and a professional astronomer on the staff of McDonald Observatory. He also serves on the advisory board of *Stardate* magazine.

ABOUT THE PREFACE AUTHOR

Frank Bash, Ph.D., is a professor of astronomy at The University of Texas-Austin and the director of McDonald Observatory.

ABOUT THE FOREWORD AUTHOR

David H. Levy was co-discoverer of the Shoemaker-Levy Comet, the comet that crashed into Jupiter. He is renowned as a science writer as well as a comet discoverer. His most recent book is *More Things in Heaven and Earth: Poets and Astronomers Read the Night Sky,* published by Wombat Press.